UNCONSCIOUS BIAS
IN SCHOOLS

UNCONSCIOUS BIAS IN SCHOOLS

A Developmental Approach to Exploring Race and Racism

Tracey A. Benson
Sarah E. Fiarman

Harvard Education Press
Cambridge, Massachusetts

Second Printing, 2020

Paperback ISBN 978-1-68253-369-7
Library Edition ISBN 978-1-68253-370-3

Library of Congress Cataloging-in-Publication Data

Names: Benson, Tracey A., author. | Fiarman, Sarah E. (Sarah Edith), author.
Title: Unconscious bias in schools : a developmental approach to exploring
   race and racism / Tracey A. Benson, Sarah E. Fiarman.
Description: Cambridge, Massachusetts : Harvard Education Press, [2019] |
   Includes bibliographical references and index.
Identifiers: LCCN 2019014638| ISBN 9781682533697 (pbk.) | ISBN 9781682533703
   (library edition)
Subjects: LCSH: Racism in education—United States. | Educational
   equalization—United States. | Discrimination in education—United States.
   | African Americans—Education—United States. | Multicultural
   education—United States. | United States—Race relations.
Classification: LCC LC212.2 .B46 2019 | DDC 371.829/96073—dc23
LC record available at https://lccn.loc.gov/2019014638

Published by Harvard Education Press,
an imprint of the Harvard Education Publishing Group

Harvard Education Press
8 Story Street
Cambridge, MA 02138

Cover Design: Wilcox Design
Cover Image: iStock.com/Akrain
The typefaces used in this book are Adobe Garamond Pro and Futura Standard

Contents

Dedicated to courageous educators—
past, present, and future

Foreword

Having partnered over the last quarter of a century with a broad range of school districts and organizations in the United States and abroad, I have learned that schools cannot achieve racial equity without explicitly naming race and exposing racism as central in the failure to effectively serve the student groups that comprise the majority of the school population. I have also learned that educational systems' personnel are deeply challenged to examine their collective and personal beliefs about the intersection of race and that failure. At the same time, black, brown, Southeast Asian, and indigenous children continue to deserve and require qualified and skilled teachers who love instead of fear them, and who understand, value, and affirm their rich African American, Latino/a, indigenous, Asian, and other cultures.

In *Unconscious Bias in Schools: A Developmental Approach to Exploring Race and Racism*, Tracey Benson and Sarah Fiarman, through their own personal and professional experiences, acknowledge and seek to address what these stark racial truths look, sound, and feel like in schools. Through their practice as school principals and coaches for those aspiring to be the same, they've encountered numerous occasions where racial bias was clearly playing a role in the treatment of certain student and adult populations. However, at times, they did not have the necessary resources to help address these issues effectively.

In this book, Tracey and Sarah set out to fill this gap. They reflect upon and share insights and practices. They both acknowledge and know, viscerally and intuitively, the racial context in which they learn, teach, and lead, and seek to guide teachers and principals to acquire and practice the racial consciousness and literacy required to transform the structures, culture, and climate of schools and classrooms. Educators, at all levels, need to learn how to talk about race. We must develop a proficient level of literacy and competence about the racial context in which we are *all* socialized and its history and evolution to the present, and in our inherited and emerging relationships with one another. It is vital that educators examine, interrupt, and dismantle how racism is institutionalized in schooling and the role that plays in creating, maintaining, and perpetuating racial disparities. The resultant inequity is systemic, predictable and disproportionate by race, and reflective of opportunity, experience, and attainment writ large in education and society.

Unconscious Bias in Schools: A Developmental Approach to Exploring Race and Racism provides a historical and contemporary understanding of racial bias in schools as a side effect of centuries of US racism. This volume also offers suggestions on how to prepare, as a school leader, to dive into these issues within the school and specific strategies to employ to root out the mass and vestiges of racial bias in the school as a whole, as well as in the classroom. The hope is that school leaders will incorporate strategies put forward herein to increase principal and teacher efficacy, transform the culture and improve the climate of schools, and increase student achievement.

Leadership development for racial equity is at the core of this book. Benson and Fiarman are avid practitioners of Courageous Conversation, advocates for social justice, and committed anti-racist leaders. *Courageous Conversations About Race: A Field Guide to Achieving Equity in Schools*, 2nd ed., is referenced as an important resource in carrying out this work in schools. Many of the school-based examples provide specific strategies and next steps for schools that are engaged in this work.

I hope that *Unconscious Bias in Schools: A Developmental Approach to Exploring Race and Racism* empowers you to engage in, sustain, and deepen interracial dialogue about race in your schools and other personal, professional, and organizational settings. I am optimistic that together we can and will work to transform the culture and climate of silence about the racial context and experience that is schooling in the United States. The construction of race is acknowledged, documented, studied, and understood. The evidence and impact are irrefutable. Overcoming the inability and/or lack of will to name, talk about, and examine racism in every aspect of our social order and system of schooling born of, practiced, and sophisticated in race must be a function of transformed belief, conscious intent, and explicit action. May this book be a useful contribution to your practice of each.

Glenn E. Singleton
Founder and President
Courageous Conversation
Pacific Educational Group

Introduction

Early in our collaboration, when we were working with aspiring principals, Tracey sent Sarah an email that made her sit up and take notice. We were both members of the teaching team in the School Leadership Program at Harvard Graduate School of Education. Tracey was a doctoral student seeking to work with school leaders, and Sarah was a new lecturer in the program. In the two months we had been working together, this was the first time we had had an exchange like the one in that email.

We were reflecting with our teaching colleagues on an intense, all-day workshop that our students had co-led and co-facilitated. During the workshop, students had broken into racial affinity groups and then reported back to the whole group on their discussions, which included feelings of frustration, anger, defensiveness, shame, fear, resignation, and pride. As a teaching team, we were considering the question of whether we should plan a structured debriefing of the experience. Tracey felt that it would send the wrong message to students. He felt that we needed to demonstrate to students that conversations about race are a normal part of our work as educators. For this reason, we shouldn't treat these conversations differently than we would treat any other conversation. Rather than stopping to debrief each time, we should just keep having them. When Sarah disagreed with this approach, Tracey's email reply pointed out that in a discussion about how to process a workshop about race, shouldn't a white woman seek to understand a black man's dissent first before disagreeing with it?

The directness of the email brought Sarah up short. She immediately realized that (a) Tracey was right, and (b) this was not a conversation for email. In her reply, Sarah agreed and asked if they could meet. Thus, on a gray Sunday afternoon, the two of us met on a mostly empty campus for a conversation

1

that made both of us anxious. Tracey remembers assuming that he would likely be kicked off the teaching team. He knew the email would generate a response, and he had thought long and hard before pressing "send." He finally told himself he was tired of choosing the safe action, the action that wouldn't rock the boat. Continually muffling his real thoughts in order to preserve harmony was exhausting. He wanted to be able to express how he felt without self-censoring.

In her work as a teacher and principal, Sarah was used to black families and colleagues seeing her as an ally. She'd taken the job at Harvard on the condition that she could infuse discussions of race and racism into all coursework, from budgets to supervision. In weekly planning meetings for class, Tracey had been a valuable collaborator. He regularly suggested lesson plan ideas that led to probing, meaningful reflection in class. While Tracey's email was hard to read, she knew there was a great deal to learn from his feedback.

On that October afternoon at the school library, we formed a partnership. Tracey took time to meet with Sarah during a week when by all accounts he had no time to spare. Sitting across a table with a tall cup of coffee in front of him, he placed his laptop and books aside and answered Sarah's questions with patience and in detail. He asked repeatedly, "Is there anything else you want to ask about?" Despite the pull of schoolwork that needed to be completed, he remained until she'd asked her last question. After the meeting, Sarah thanked Tracey and then went home and did something Tracey had never experienced from a white person before. She wrote up what she'd heard and the insights she'd gained from listening to Tracey and emailed him to let him know what he had taught her and to ensure she hadn't misheard him.

Over the course of the year, we (Tracey and Sarah) formed a friendship. We were both former principals who missed teaching. In between grading papers and planning for our class, we reminisced together about the challenges of supervision, discovered we had both felt like horrified grandparents when chaperoning the school dance, and compared war stories about that single teacher who had resisted change the most. Few people understand the experience of being a principal, and it was reassuring to hear that we'd faced so many similar challenges.

We also formed a connection over our common concern that the US school system does not serve all students equally well. Too many black and brown students in this country are deprived of a quality education. This injustice is what drew each of us to education and eventually into school leadership. We wanted to lead schools that would break the pattern, provide excellent teaching, and produce equally high levels of performance for students of all racial backgrounds. Even though our schools had been very different—one a more traditional high school, the other a progressive elementary school—our goals were the same. As school leaders, we saw ourselves as foot soldiers in the ongoing civil rights movement.

Looking back on our time as principals, we feel proud of the work we did at our respective schools, indebted to inspired teacher leaders who championed this work with us, and humbled by the complexity of the work. While we each saw growth that made students, teachers, and parents proud, we both also recognized that we didn't have all the answers. In particular, we didn't have all the answers for how to help our schools directly address racism and its impact on our students and ourselves. We wished that instead of learning through trial and error, we'd been given some guidance on this subject or, frankly, even just one example to follow.

Looking back, we can see that the key lesson we needed to understand—and that we've been trying to convey to principals since then—is that reducing the effects of racism on students requires deep change in how educators view themselves and their work. In the language of change management, this is an adaptive rather than a technical challenge.[1] Adaptive challenges require changing mindsets rather than simply skill sets. Rather than define our schools as bias free, we need to start from the opposite assumption. Despite our very best intentions, racial bias is alive and well in schools. If we as educators are not addressing this bias, it will undermine the progress educators are trying to make. To reduce the effects of racism on students, we all need to create an environment where teachers and administrators can talk openly and courageously about race, identify where racial bias interferes with school goals, and take decisive actions to uncover, address, and eliminate the impact of racial bias from school systems, policies, and practices.

This is the guidance we wanted to provide as we entered our roles as instructors in a school leadership program. We wanted to help our students—aspiring principals—learn from our strengths as leaders for increasing racially equitable outcomes, but we also wanted our students to learn from what we wished we'd done better—opportunities missed and hard lessons learned. With our teaching colleagues, we planned lessons on the history of explicit racist policies that have created racially segregated schools, how to work on our own personal racial identity development, how to have courageous conversations about race with colleagues, and how to conduct root cause analyses of racially disparate learning outcomes.

As graduation approached and our students accepted school leader positions around the United States, we reflected on the year, together with our teaching team. In particular, we considered whether our students were prepared to combat racism at their future schools. We concluded that we couldn't be sure. We didn't have clear evidence of skill development across the cohort. We should have required more concrete application of the skills we discussed, more practice. We also grappled with the question of whether we were reaching everyone, especially the students in our class who were silent during discussions about race. Even with those who were most engaged, we weren't confident that we'd given them the tools they needed to help their faculties deeply examine, understand, and address the racial inequities at their schools. This recognition ultimately led to us collaborating on a book to fill this void in the field.

Shortly after our students graduated, Tracey proposed that we continue to have regular conversations about how to help school leaders address racism in their schools. Tracey was moving to serve alongside principal supervisors in the Houston Independent School District, while Sarah continued teaching aspiring principals at Harvard. Our pattern was to talk on the phone while Tracey was driving home in traffic and Sarah walked laps around a local track.

In one early conversation, as Sarah was stumbling over her words, Tracey said, "Sarah, there's this thing that white people do—this dance—when they are worried they're going to say something racist. You're doing that now. Don't worry. I already know you're racist. And I think the world of you. So just say it." Sarah understood she had internalized racism—that she couldn't escape it in the deeply racist society we live in—but it was still startling to hear this so directly from Tracey.

It was this frankness that helped us—and continues to help us—learn from each other. Sarah shares her raw thoughts openly with Tracey and listens closely as he describes his experiences. As a black man with experience teaching white people about racism, Tracey understands race, racism, and whiteness. His questions and patience help Sarah notice the ways her perspective has been shaped by a lifetime of societal messages that establish whiteness as the norm and everything else as less than or other. He doesn't hesitate to point out her internalized racism and to tell her how difficult their conversations can be for him as well.

Tracey values Sarah's perspective because, in his experience, he does not often get the opportunity to hear the unfiltered, inner thoughts of white people on topics of race and racism. He used to think that white people were intentionally holding back in conversations about race, but through many unfiltered conversations about race with Sarah, he's come to understand that many white people truly don't believe they have something to contribute to conversations about race. They're not putting up a front. They honestly don't see themselves as having a racial identity. He has also come to realize through these conversations that white people can find dialogues about race and racism very intimidating and anxiety producing, especially when they are in racially heterogeneous settings, out of intense fear of saying the wrong thing, looking ignorant or, even worse, being seen as racist.

Over the years, our conversations haven't exclusively focused on race. We've heard about each other's families and college exploits. We've also learned about each other's quirks and habits. After hearing about Sarah's irregular vacuuming and dusting schedule, Tracey confessed to being a neat freak and warned he would have to don a space suit before coming over for brunch. At the same time, he also confessed to enjoying the local Zombie 5K race where he and other runners got splattered with mud and fake blood. Looking over Tracey's shoulder as he perused his Facebook page, Sarah gasped when she saw a picture that included a former boyfriend . . . getting married. After Tracey's wife put him on a vegan diet, Tracey and Sarah bonded over tempeh and buffalo cauliflower. Sarah learned that Tracey and his wife have an unusual number of shoes, when she helped them with last-minute packing on their way to spend the summer abroad. Tracey responded to Sarah's last-minute plea for editing help from a café in New York City during a family vacation.

As we've worked together, we've noticed some common patterns we hear when talking to school leaders about racism. White leaders fear being seen as racist. Leaders of color fear the backlash from defensive white people. People of color like Tracey usually have their guard up from too many conversations that go poorly and end up with everyone tending to a distraught white person, while the ongoing, daily struggles of the people of color go unnoticed. White people like Sarah typically enter these conversations on the defensive.

As Sarah can attest, she's often spent whole meetings trying to prove she's not racist while on tenterhooks the entire time for fear she'll say something that indicates she is. With everyone's defenses up, it's no wonder that most educators enter these conversations with nervousness and sometimes dread.

A HELPFUL APPROACH

Over the years, we have discovered a concept that can shift these dynamics: unconscious racial bias. This is the concept that, throughout our daily lives, we all absorb and internalize prejudices that influence our automatic actions and beliefs. The absorption of these biases is not a conscious process and in fact, can run counter to what we think we believe. Framing our work with the concept of unconscious racial bias allows us to decouple intention from racism. It allows us to focus on what's most important: the impact on students. An understanding of this concept provides an opening where we've previously seen only closed doors. The two of us have found that when we teach about unconscious racial bias, many white people are more willing to engage, stay in the conversation, and consider the possibility that their behaviors might unintentionally cause harm to students. In this context, white people we've worked with seem able to move past guilt and shame to a more productive perspective. People of color benefit from a deeper understanding of unconscious racial bias because, as with white colleagues, people of color have also absorbed the same negative images and social cues that produce a preference for the "socially valued group."

We believe that unconscious racial bias *is* unconscious racism. However, we also recognize that "racism" is such a loaded term that it is not a helpful starting place for conversation. Putting educators on the defensive isn't a winning strategy for helping people learn. While we believe white people need to be able to talk about racism and the ways they directly benefit within a racist society, we also believe this is a developmental process. Language can be a barrier. If the phrase "unconscious bias" allows more people to enter the conversation, we're going to use it.

Are there downsides to using the phrase "unconscious bias" instead of "racism"? There are. Naming this as an "unconscious" process may allow white people to feel they can absolve themselves of responsibility and urgency to engage in anti-bias work: "I can't help it. These biases are in my unconscious."

We all risk falling into the trap of what researcher Bonilla-Silva calls "racism without racists."[2] In addition, framing the concept of bias as implicating everyone *equally* erases the differential ways that racism affects white people and people of color. White people can choose to walk away from the topic and remain personally unscathed. People of color, on the other hand, do not have such a luxury; they will be directly disadvantaged by bias in their daily lives. So, while we've all internalized racial bias, the outcomes of this bias affect us in very different ways.

At the end of the day, as two people responsible for teaching school leaders, we're pragmatists. We have one clear goal: to eliminate the negative impacts of racial bias on all students. Black and brown students feel the impact directly. White students absorb the unconscious bias as bystanders from adults they've come to trust. Like many principals, we are concerned for students and urgently seek a solution.

Most teachers in the United States are white. Many white people shut down when discussing racism. We're looking for a strategy that works, not an opportunity to make a statement. Teaching about the unconscious nature of racial bias provides a valuable entry point into a conversation that most schools simply do not have. We've seen this approach unlock doors that have been slammed shut, and we want to share this key that we found to be helpful.

As we've moved into new professional roles, we continue to pursue this work—Tracey as a professor of educational leadership, and Sarah in developing and supporting school principals around the country. We've led workshops on addressing unconscious racial bias based on the ideas in this book. At one point, when we co-presented about this topic at a workshop for administrators and their higher-education professors, participants kept jumping up to take pictures of our PowerPoint slides. We were a little taken aback (our graphics weren't *that* good) and marveled at it later. However, it confirmed what we had been experiencing in other settings. School leaders want to address racial inequities in schools and don't know how. They're looking for guidance. The concept of unconscious bias can serve as a valuable tool.

We wrote this book to support the leaders we continue to meet who seek to interrupt the patterns of racial inequity at their schools and who feel isolated in that endeavor. We want to share the lessons we've learned that we wish someone had shared with us when we were entering the principalship. We don't have all the answers. We still regularly engage in very uncomfortable and courageous conversations with each other to deepen our racial understand-ings. It's hard work. We're glad to be in it together and invite our readers to join us in this community.

WHAT'S IN OUR BOOK

We did not write a how-to book. We do not prescribe a specific set of direc-tions. The following chapters do, however, provide an order of operations. To determine that order, we worked backward. To reduce the impact of rac-ism in our schools, school leaders need to create the conditions for faculty to talk about race and their own unconscious racial biases. This requires that school communities name and discuss race with the explicit intent of learning together rather than judging each other. Chapters 1 through 5 describe the conditions and skill building necessary for teachers to productively examine data to identify where racial bias is impacting student learning. In chapters 6 through 8, we describe ways to examine school climate and academics for signs of bias. The goal of these chapters is to help readers develop a mindset of inquiry into racial bias in the same way that effective teachers continu-ally examine their reading or math practice for ways to get better. Thus, we recommend processes for ongoing inquiry rather than specific solutions to implement. In chapter 9, we discuss some of the common hurdles and pitfalls of examining data and the ways biases show up in this seemingly objective endeavor. We round out the book with a discussion about how to sustain the work in the long term, which includes addressing resistance, maintaining a growth mindset, and practicing self-care.

A Detailed Outline of the Book

Chapter 1 provides an overview of unconscious racial bias and its impact on multiple sectors of our society. School leaders are better equipped to address current racial inequalities when they understand their history and how racial bias continues to influence student outcomes. Research shows that people of color continue to be systematically deprived of equal opportunity to acquire and/or accumulate wealth, health, safety, and education. While some of this is due to conscious racism, increasingly researchers document the ways in which people discriminate based on race without consciously seeking to do so. Chapter 1 includes examples of unconscious racial bias across our society, including in education. It's undeniable; unconscious bias negatively impacts students.

How do leaders help their schools reduce the effects of unconscious racial bias? We recommend leaders first examine their own mindset. Without this step, leaders might leap into action, committed to tackling racial inequalities in their schools only to be jolted backward or off course when first attempts don't go well. In order to gain the persistence and mindset necessary to do this work, we all need to engage in the deeply introspective and at times unsettling work of examining how we view ourselves and the educators we work with. Most of us have internalized the idea that people fall into two categories: racists with malicious intentions or nonracists who are the rest of us. We refer to this as the racist/nonracist binary. Confronting this binary in ourselves helps us free others from this mindset.

In chapter 2, we describe this racist/nonracist binary and how this duality plays out in our work as leaders. We use ourselves as exhibit A. We describe how this binary mindset shows up in a conversation about students and threatens to disrupt progress and collaboration. Before leaders can help others, they first need to tackle this deep-rooted binary mindset in themselves. In this way, they learn to see themselves and colleagues as learners on a continuum of growth instead of as either racists or nonracists.

Once leaders understand the ways their own mindsets influence their leadership in addressing racism, they can turn to the work of supporting their staff in this work. One question a leader can begin with is, "What is my school's capacity to talk about race?" For most white teachers around the country, race is a taboo subject. Talking about race in mixed-race settings simply isn't common for people of any racial background, so leaders need to start by building these skills. Chapter 3 describes the ways most educators typically avoid talking about race in schools and the importance of making it a normal, everyday practice. A central practice in this effort is working on racial identity development. Exploring our varied racial identities is a critical antidote to the false concept of colorblindness.

As with any significant school improvement effort and especially for efforts pertaining to race, success hinges on the culture leaders establish at their school. Strong leaders cultivate communities where people speak their truths, face their flaws, and count on their colleagues to do the same. In chapter 4, we describe what is involved in cultivating this culture so educators can face and address racial bias together.

Regardless of racial background, few of us have experience giving and getting feedback about unconscious racial bias, and even fewer have experience that is positive. This poses a considerable challenge for a leader. When a leader can't describe or picture what success looks like, knowing what moves will get there is challenging. In chapter 4, we share a vision of what it looks like when community members are able to talk directly to each other about their biases. It's inspiring to witness. We also examine a few common pitfalls that these "brave communities" and their leaders will likely face.

Chapter 5 describes one of the most common forms of resistance in this work: the need to keep white people comfortable. Principals and others leading this work need to be particularly aware of the ways that they may be pulled into centering white people's comfort and, in so doing, avoid some of the hard conversations that need to happen. Centering white comfort manifests in a variety of ways. People in positions of power may simply never get around to scheduling the work or may never empower others to lead it. Some white people may avoid facing their racial biases by shutting down in conversations, or by maintaining the conversation at a superficial level. Leaders need courage to recognize and face resistance firmly and clearly. They also need to be alert to the fact that the resistance may not just come from their staff; it may also come from within themselves.

In chapters 6 through 8, we describe a variety of places to look for the impact of racial bias. Some readers may balk at this approach. Why would you fish around for bad news? However, we already know there's bad news. Everyone in school buildings has breathed in the smog of unconscious racial bias. We start with the assumption that while it may be unwanted, it is alive and well in all schools. The goal for educators is find out where and how it may be influencing their work. To do this, we examine data about students' experiences and learning in school. Chapters 6 through 8 provide examples of the types of data educators might collect regarding school climate, classroom climate and instruction, and overall academic program.

Educators need data for two reasons: to help us see the biases we don't realize we have and can't see on our own and to help us monitor whether the changes made in practice actually lead to improved outcomes for students. While awareness stimulates motivation to make changes, data measure whether in fact those changes are making a difference. What ultimately matters is not how enlightened we are as educators but rather the impact our actions have on the students we serve.

Throughout the process of examining data, educators need to be alert to the ways biases can influence interpretations of the findings. Chapter 9 describes the difference framing can make. Too often, we all let ourselves off the hook. We have a choice. We can see student achievement data as a reflection of innate student capacity or as a sign that something in teacher practice isn't hitting the mark. This chapter addresses the tendency to distance ourselves from the problem and instead place blame on students. As with other improvement efforts, addressing unconscious racial bias requires that educators cultivate a collective sense of ownership and develop the capacity to take personal responsibility for their impact. The way leaders frame the problem matters.

Finally, this work is challenging and ongoing, with. We need a plan for the long game. The final chapter includes strategies for maintaining momentum over time. In the face of resistance, it can be tempting to doubt our skills and direction. It is helpful to remember that this work is a developmental process and we're going to need to crawl before we walk. One strategy that leaders can't forget is the need for self-care. We each need to find a trusted colleague who can listen, help us problem solve, and most of all, sustain us.

Throughout the book, we reference articles and authors whose work we've used in workshops and classes. We include many of these in a list of suggested resources at the end of the book. We hope the list provides some initial ideas for readers who want to explore this work more deeply, as well as some useful texts or videos appropriate for use in meetings at school with staff. It is by no means comprehensive but rather serves as a jumping-off point for discovering the right resources for your own learning and that of your staff.

A SPOTLIGHT ON RACIAL BIAS

While biases exist about many different aspects of identity, this book focuses exclusively on racial bias. This is not because we think other forms of bias are less important. We know that no single aspect of identity can ever be completely separated from other aspects. There's merit in understanding the range of biases and the ways they intersect—black girls experience bias in a different way from black boys, gay Latino boys experience biases that straight Latino boys do not, and so on. Intersectionality is a critically important concept worthy of investigation and reflection.

However, what we've noticed is that when people consider race within the context of multiple identities, they often avoid it or give it a very light touch at best. Most educators—most Americans—do not have experience talking about race and particularly the impacts of racism within mixed-race, professional settings. This lack of experience, combined with what many feel is a loaded topic, may explain why people so often avoid discussing this aspect of intersectional identities. Over and over, we've seen groups avoid talking about race when given the option to examine other aspects of their identity. This dance of avoidance would be humorous to watch if it weren't so damaging.

This avoidance has consequences. *Achievement and opportunity gaps disproportionately affect students of color.* For this reason, we've chosen to focus this book exclusively on racial bias. However, the methods of exploring and addressing bias that we describe in this book are applicable to a range of biases. We expect that deepening expertise about unconscious racial bias will help educators see the importance of examining a full range of biases.

The examples in this book come from a range of schools. Many are from the different schools where we each served as principal. When we draw from our past experiences as leaders—each at more than one school—we have tried to ensure that the people we mention individually are not recognizable, even to themselves.[3] Other examples are from schools we've visited or leaders we've interviewed, taught, worked with, or supported in some way. In several chapters, we highlight examples from one school, Capital City Public Charter School in Washington, DC. The leaders of this school have a clear vision and laser-like focus on engaging staff in ongoing racial identity development and discussions of the impact of racial bias. We think seeing multiple examples from this school's approach provides a valuable model.

Principals rarely talk to each other about race, let alone principals with different racial identities. As coauthors, we've been reaping the rewards from the conversations with each other for several years, and we want to share that with school leaders. We hope reading this book feels like joining a conversation with two passionate colleagues who tell it like it is. Through the ups and downs of leadership, we've longed for like-minded colleagues. We're glad you've chosen to learn with us.

CHAPTER 1

Do We Have a Bias Problem?

As a teacher, Sarah noticed one year that her black students were having frequent side conversations during her class. When she mentioned this to a black colleague, he pointed out that she might be falling into a common pattern. Educators, he suggested, frequently notice misbehavior among black students while ignoring the same behavior among white students. Sure enough, when Sarah observed more carefully in her next class, white students were doing the same thing. Without realizing it, Sarah had selectively noticed the misbehavior of just one subset of students. As someone who cares about equity, teaches about racism, and leads an anti-racism faculty group, how could she have read the situation so inaccurately? How could she have shown such bias?

Just a few years earlier, Tracey had a similar revelation when he was a high school principal carrying out hallway duty in between classes. A black student complained that Tracey and other staff members were treating black students differently than white students in the hallways during passing time. One black student said to Tracey during a conversation in his office, "Why are you all always picking on us? How come when we are standing and talking with our friends—just like the white students—not causing any trouble, you or some teacher comes over to us and tells us to get to class?" After this conversation with the student, Tracey spent the next week just observing in the hallways between classes. His informal data collection confirmed the student was right. Faculty and staff were consistently ignoring white students who congregated in the hallways between classes and redirecting black and brown students who were engaging in the same behavior. Like Sarah, Tracey was alarmed to recognize that he'd been treating black students unfairly; however, unlike Sarah, he was not surprised. As a black man in America, he knew to expect racial bias from even the most unlikely places.

For the two of us as school leaders, these instances revealing our own racial biases gave us pause. In these separate incidents, each of us had viewed black students as troublemakers and had granted white students leniency. We were disturbed to realize that we cannot trust our instincts. We were also deeply concerned to consider how frequently students of color experience this kind of increased surveillance and suspicion from well-meaning adults responsible for their education. Consider the impact this must have on the psyche of a young person.

Research shows that examples like these happen many times every day in schools. Racial bias is present in our schools. In both small and also significant ways, the treatment students and parents of color receive is different from the treatment white students and families receive.[1] What makes this hard to grasp is that the vast majority of us as educators care about our students—students of all racial backgrounds. However, in countless decisions throughout the day, we are in positions to erode a child's self-image, dampen a child's curiosity, burden a student with low expectations, and cause a child to feel inferior, inadequate, or otherwise lacking.

Educators perpetrating these harmful acts are often those who care deeply about their students' welfare. Both of us have come to recognize our role in perpetuating this pattern of unequal treatment of students of color. Through our experiences, we know how vital it is for school leaders to recognize the role they play in inequality and to help their staff members do the same. In this chapter, we explore the fundamentals of unconscious racial bias. Recognizing this new manifestation of racism is the first step in addressing its influence on ourselves and its impact on students. We explain what it is and where it comes from. Then we show some of the negative impact of unconscious racial bias on different sectors of our society, including education.

RACISM DOESN'T SHUT OFF LIKE A LIGHT SWITCH

As a black man, Tracey usually can't go through a day without people treating him differently because of his skin color. The treatment is often subtle but still there. White people regularly cross the street when he's approaching. Passengers leave a berth of empty seats around him on crowded trains. The cashier at the grocery store says hello to everyone else in line but "Wassup?" to him. His principal mentor advises him to never meet with a white teacher alone in his office because if anyone accuses him of improper action, his testimony will never hold up in the predominantly white community. Before he says a word, people view Tracey with suspicion and fear.

Most white people would find this day-to-day experience hard to imagine. Recently, Tracey came back from a community meeting addressing school integration and exclaimed, "They just don't get it! These are good white people—really *good* people—and they have no idea what people of color experience in this community." This is part of the problem. Most white educators find it hard to understand how significantly racism impacts students every day.

We can't quickly reverse centuries of history. For hundreds of years in the United States, people of color have been denied their full humanity, removed from their land, enslaved, denied basic rights, and oppressed by state-sanctioned violence and theft. For nearly half a millennium, white people in this country have granted themselves privileges that they simultaneously denied people of color—policies that grant land, housing, education, voting rights, policies designed to increase the prosperity of white people while systematically denying these same rights to people of color. We would be naive to think that a society's deeply held racism—codified into laws, enforced by judges and law enforcement, taught explicitly and passed on implicitly in homes and schools—can be turned off like a light switch. It can't.

It is certainly true that our country has made progress. We've seen remarkable improvements for people of color in basic civil rights, increasing representation, and access to power. These are worth celebrating. Yet, the daily experiences of many people of color continue to be negatively impacted by both the vestiges of historical racism and the contemporary manifestations of racism.

Racism today looks different from the racism of fifty years ago. We don't always recognize it. Most of us readily condemn overt bigotry. But the fact is that racism hasn't been eliminated. In some ways, it's gone underground to live in our collective unconscious. School leaders committed to continuing the work of the civil rights movement must turn their attention to what is called the "new racism": *unconscious racial bias*.

WHAT IS UNCONSCIOUS RACIAL BIAS?

Recent headlines from the *New York Times, Harvard Business Review,* and *Fortune* magazine blared, "Who me, biased?" "7 Practical Ways to Reduce Bias in Your Hiring," "How Unconscious Bias is Holding Your Company Back."[2] From presidential debates to corporate headquarters across the country, the concept of unconscious bias (also called "implicit bias") has been in the spotlight. We're learning that as Americans, we harbor negative biases about old people, women, Muslims, Jews, people with disabilities, people of color, and other aspects of our identities. Nearly every major media outlet has run segments on this phenomenon, which also features regularly in business magazines.

Unconscious bias is often explained as a rational phenomenon, an inherent characteristic of being human. We can't process all the information we're constantly taking in, so our mind relies on shortcuts. We make associations rather than individually considering each situation. These shortcuts happen so quickly, we're usually not aware we're using them. They're *unconscious.* While some associations are harmless, others are not. As a video series in the *New York Times* explained, unconsciously associating the words "peanut butter" with the word "jelly" doesn't hurt anyone.[3] However, when we think of a black person and unconsciously associate that person with "criminal," our unconscious biases have negative effects that potentially harm real people. Educators, as professionals who make hundreds if not thousands of decisions before lunchtime, need to be aware of how unconscious racial biases influence them.

Our definition of unconscious racial bias for the purposes of this book is *learned beliefs, attitudes, and stereotypes about a particular race that result in harmful or preferential treatment of members of that race.* As with anything unconscious, this type of racial bias has nothing to do with conscious intentions, because the thoughts and actions are not known to the conscious mind. Unconscious racial bias is a cognitive process that has been built over time from constant societal exposure to racially biased imagery, narratives, and depictions. This exposure happens daily, just beyond the conscious mind, from the moment people wake up to the moment they go to sleep at night. These constant messages prime the brain to prefer certain races of people over others.

A growing body of research shows that we all harbor unconscious biases. Tests of *implicit bias* (or unconscious bias) show that people of all backgrounds show unconscious preferences on the basis of gender, race, sexual orientation, or other aspects of identity. The most cited research comes from the implicit-association test at Harvard University.[4] In 1998, professors Mahzarin Banaji, Anthony Greenwald, and Brian Nosek designed a test that requires people to make quick decisions associating positive and negative qualities with people of different races. (The study measures associations with a variety of other identities such as religion, gender, LGBTQ status, age, and more.) Thousands of people have taken the test. According to these tests and others like them, most people favor the group they are a member of, despite their claims that they have no preference. The tests also show, however, that people across groups show preferences for the "culturally valued group." Approximately one-third to one-half of people in "stigmatized groups" tend to favor the culturally valued group.[5] Researchers found that even when people stated that they harbored no prejudice against people of color, most showed a tendency to associate people of color with negative characteristics.

Perhaps what is most surprising is that these biases influence us even when they are in direct opposition to our espoused beliefs—and sometimes in opposition to our own lived experience. That's because unconscious biases are just that—*unconscious*. As psychologist Beverly Daniel Tatum explains, we absorb bias in the same way we breathe in smog—involuntarily and usually without any awareness of it.[6] We're similarly unaware of how they influence our behavior.

A Note About Race

Before we go further, it's important to note that the very notion of race is a socially constructed concept. Our country's history of racial oppression includes supposedly "scientific" treatises on the existence of different races and the differences between these races. Many educators are unaware that Irish and Italian people in the nineteenth century were not considered to be white. Despite the fact that the very definitions of race have shifted over time, the theory of a biological concept of race has persisted. These theories have maintained a firm hold on the psyche of most Americans, even as they've been disproven repeatedly in recent decades.

Most Americans are surprised to learn that contemporary genetic research has proven that there *is no genetic category of race*. In reality, genetic differences are more likely to be found *within* what we think of as a racial group than across these groups. In other words, a white woman could have more genes in common with a black woman than with another white person.[7] As bioengineering professor Ian Holmes points out, genetic differences may be associated with ancestry but ancestry is not the same as race as we have come to define it in American society.[8] Even as we refer to race in this book, we're aware that it is a social and not a biological concept. This social construction has stuck, however. It now forms the underpinnings of unconscious racial bias.

WHERE DOES UNCONSCIOUS RACIAL BIAS COME FROM?

We're not born with unconscious racial bias. We learn it. Understanding how we learn this unconscious process helps us address it. Biases of all kinds can be at least partly explained by our families and experiences. After all, our families shape many of our worldviews. Parents who harbor biases tend to pass them on to the next generation, sometimes explicitly and directly, other times through more subtle means like body language or patterns of behavior. When a parent's body stiffens as a person of a different race enters the elevator, the child makes the association. When parents and teachers avoid talking about race, children learn there's something taboo there. When parents' friends are all of the same race, children learn lessons about who fits into their particular social circle. These associations become intuitive rather than rational. However, there are also systematic ways that racial bias infiltrates the unconscious.

An Ignorance of History

Many people falsely assume that current racial disparities in areas such as income and educational level are the result of individual choices and behaviors rather than understanding the role history plays in the current reality. This ignorance of history allows racial bias to develop unchecked in our unconscious. We interpret racial inequalities as a natural rather than a manmade outcome.

Most people are familiar with contemporary patterns of racial inequality: black people, on average, have lower net worth than white people. There are fewer black and brown professionals who hold graduate degrees than white professionals. A disproportionate percentage of people of color live in poverty. And, there are fewer black people who own their own homes than white people. All of the above may appear to be a natural occurrence—something inherent to black people. Statistics like these might lead someone to assume that black and brown people are simply not as ambitious or hardworking as white people. As historians know, however, the current reality is not a natural occurrence at all. These disparities are the result of explicit policies over many generations that have prevented black people from accumulating wealth, education, and property, while explicitly protecting and increasing support for white people to advance in those same areas.

In his book *The Color of Law: A Forgotten History of How Our Government Segregated America*, economist Richard Rothstein documents in detail the ways zoning policies, federal subsidies, urban planning commissions, and federal and local laws deliberately excluded people of color.[9] These systems and structures created segregated communities, underfunded schools, and generations of poverty. It's not happenstance that homeownership is lower among African Americans than whites, but rather the result of explicit policies intended to produce a desired outcome.

As one example, the benefits of the GI Bill such as subsidized housing, loans, and higher education for war veterans are often credited with creating a strong middle class. However, the bill did not serve black and white veterans equally. The bill effectively excluded black veterans from reaping benefits because the federally backed banking industry refused to extend loans to black people. This prevented generations of black families from accumulating wealth, while the government granted white peers access to subsidized loans and newly developed suburban housing, which led to increasing net worth over time.

Explicitly discriminatory mortgage policies led to increasingly segregated communities. This practice resulted in the devaluing of property in predominantly black and brown neighborhoods because banks wouldn't approve loans to buy there. The lagging property value resulted in more poorly funded schools and decreased access to healthy food as supermarkets moved to the suburbs where the middle class expanded, thanks to the same federal banking policies that excluded people of color.

In an investigative report on contemporary housing policy, reporter Nikole Hannah-Jones summarized the significance of segregated housing: "[For] every measure of well-being and opportunity, the foundation is where you live . . . cancer rates, asthma rates, infant mortality, unemployment, education, access to fresh food, access to parks, whether or not the city repairs the roads in your neighborhood."[10] And Rothstein affirms the impact of twentieth-century housing policies: "Our system of official segregation was not the result of a single law that consigned African Americans to designated neighborhoods. Rather scores of racially explicit laws, regulations, and government practices combine to create a nationwide system of urban ghettos, surrounded by white suburbs. Private discrimination also played a role, but it would have been considerably less effective had it not been embraced and reinforced by government."[11]

Explicit housing discrimination is not just a thing of the past. Recently, there has been a spate of lawsuits and settlements for contemporary redlining practices in some of the largest housing markets in the country. In 2015, Hudson City Savings Bank paid $33 million to settle a lawsuit filed by the Consumer Financial Protection Bureau and the Justice Department. From 2009 to 2013, the bank had avoided working with Latinos/as and African Americans. According to the *New York Times*, "Federal officials said it was the largest settlement in the history of both departments for redlining, the practice in which banks choke off lending to minority communities."[12] In the same year, the Department of Housing and Urban Development announced a $200 million settlement with another bank for denying mortgages to black and Latino/a homebuyers between 2008 and 2010 in Chicago and Milwaukee.[13]

Most of us don't learn this history, let alone the contemporary version of it. Explicit racist policies continue to produce much of the inequality we see around us. In a similar way, we can deconstruct other contemporary racial disparities in health, employment, and wealth to show their roots in sanctioned government policies. If we don't understand this, we're likely to interpret racial disparities as a measure of the potential of people of color rather than the result of racism.

Are we saying that every black candidate who is denied a job, a mortgage, or a health test is denied because of race? Not at all. As with white candidates, applicants, and patients, plenty of people are denied because of their individual characteristics. However, the research makes clear that people of color have received and continue to receive discriminatory treatment that denies them opportunities to enter the middle class and build a financial safety net for future generations. It would be ignorant to make inferences about communities of color based on their current status. Yet, that's what we do unconsciously all the time.

Segregated Communities

Americans live in a largely segregated society. As we've discussed, this is not by happenstance. It is the result of generations of explicit discriminatory practices and reinforced by people's choices to live with those who are similar to them and distance themselves from others.

For most Americans, and especially most white Americans, the people we interact with the most on a daily basis are racially similar to us. We tend to live with people who look like us; we shop, worship, and socialize with people of our same race. A survey given in 2012 revealed just how socially segregated this country is.[14] Researchers found that fully 75 percent of white Americans do not have friends of a different race. Their social circles are exclusively white.[15] For African Americans, 67 percent do not have friends of a different race, and for Latinos/as, the percentage is 46 percent. In addition, the researchers concluded that the average white American has a friendship circle that is 91 percent white. Because of our segregated society, opportunities to interact with people of a different race don't happen naturally for most white people.

Since the clear majority of teachers in this country are white, these data are particularly relevant for school leaders to understand. Given findings like those described, school leaders should expect that most white teachers don't have personal relationships with any people of color. Racial isolation makes them more susceptible to bias. When people are surrounded with people who look like them—in their families, neighborhoods, religious institutions—when there's no firsthand experience of someone different from them, they're more likely to draw false conclusions and to make generalizations.

The Media

Because of racial isolation, most white teachers get information about people of color not from firsthand experience but from external sources, typically various forms of media—movies, news, social media, and so on. Thus, when thinking about people of a different race, they are more susceptible to the biases and omissions of mainstream society where one-dimensional, often negative stereotypes continue to get the most airtime in our national media.

In fact, we're all powerfully influenced by the media. A steady stream of messages, images, and repeated narratives from the news, movies, and advertisements are part of daily life.

Sarah discovered one way the media had influenced her when she was called to jury duty. After stating the accusations against the defendant and reading his name, the judge asked the gathered jurors, "Have any of you already made a decision about the defendant's innocence or guilt?" In that moment, before the trial had even begun, Sarah was surprised to realize she had already judged the defendant guilty. She traced her suspicion back to the moment the judge read his Italian name. Her unconscious association between Italian names and the Mafia had influenced her judgment against all reason.

One of the most persistent ways that we absorb unconscious racial bias is through what we see and hear in the media. Messages don't have to be overt or explicit. Most often, they're easily and unconsciously inferred. In the media in our society, white is what is normal. Everything else is "other."

If you are reading this and you are white, seeing people who look like you in mass media may not be something you often think about. Every day, the culture reflects not only you but nearly infinite variations of you—executives, poets, garbage collectors, soldiers, nurses, and so on. The world shows you that your possibilities are boundless.

Those of us who are not white have considerably more trouble finding any representation of ourselves in mass media and other arenas of public life, let alone representation that indicates that our humanity is multifaceted. Relating to characters on-screen is necessary not merely for us to feel seen and understood, but also for others who need to see and understand us. When it doesn't happen, we are all the poorer for it.

Constant Messages That "Normal" Means "White"

As humans, we're quick to pick up on patterns and quick to notice when something doesn't fit a given pattern. For example, supermodels define beauty for most Americans. Since the vast majority of online, catalog, and television models are white, we internalize a definition of beauty as having white features. Faces that do not have white features don't fit in that category. By normalizing white beauty, we implicitly define the physical characteristics of women of color as outside the bounds of beautiful.

Routine activities constantly expose us to messages that build our unconscious associations. We receive these messages from movies, advertisements, news sites, television, and more. Advertising depicts happy families, kids going to school, loving dog owners, and people driving expensive cars. The majority of these images depict white people. The "normal" shade for Band-Aids and mannequins is a white skin tone. Greeting cards, foods, and entertainment typically associated with white people are normal, with a separate section for "mahogany" cards, "ethnic" food, and black entertainment. A 2016 study documented the underrepresentation of people of color in film, TV, and digital production: "Over 50% of stories featured no Asian speaking characters, and 22% featured no Black or African American characters."[16] This constant, daily stream of exclusively white images, coupled with the lack of black and brown representation, significantly biases our unconscious associations with happy people, rich protagonists, and successful professionals.

While this may seem innocuous to some readers, normalization has significant implications for how we view ourselves and others. One of our basic human needs is to belong. When your identity is constantly outside what is "normal," the effect is to feel you are "other." To feel that you don't belong. The flip side of this has damaging consequences as well. White people unconsciously absorb the message that whiteness alone is normal and anything else is less than normal, doesn't belong, or is inferior. In a seminal study that focused on white children and racial preferences, researchers found that by the age of five, white children tend to attribute more positive characteristics to white people and more negative traits to black people and show a preference for having white friends over black friends.[17] In another study, even when presented with a positive narrative about a black storybook character before being asked about the attributes of the character, white children still tended to describe the black character as looking bad.[18]

These studies show that we haven't made much progress in the last sixty years. An earlier, much-cited study by Kenneth and Mamie Clark, two black psychologists who conducted the famous "doll test" in the early 1940s, found that, by the age of five, black children, when asked to choose a doll to play with, showed a preference for white dolls. The researchers also found that when asked about attributes of each doll, these children would often characterize black dolls as "looking bad" and white dolls as "nice."[19]

These studies show the deep, ongoing societal effects of racial bias in white children as well as children of color. Some of these biases are learned at home, from television, and through daily interactions with other children and adults. However, biases are also learned in schools. Thus, as educators, we have the dual task of investigating racial preferences we've absorbed throughout our lives as well as trying to lessen our role in perpetuating this pattern within our schools and classrooms.

Constant Messages That "Black" Means "Criminal"

In addition to whiteness being normalized in the media and our unconscious, black and brown people are regularly criminalized. In one report, watchdog organization Media Matters compiled studies from New York City, Los Angeles, and Pittsburgh showing that black males are disproportionately shown on the news as criminals.[20] In a 1990 study, researchers found that during one particular week of television news, of the eight times black people were the lead story, six focused exclusively on violent crimes.[21] When there were similar crime stories, the station chose to show footage of black perpetrators being led away in handcuffs, but did not include the same imagery for white perpetrators. When examining politics in the news, this same study found that news media tended to report political actions by white politicians in connection with general public interest but equated the political actions of black politicians as catered toward special interests.

These examples of the media portraying black people as violent, or only interested in serving other black people, hold enormous relevance because of the sheer number of hours of screen time Americans consume. Most polls estimate that Americans consume between twenty and forty hours of television time per week. If we add up the total hours we spend watching television, reading news online, perusing social media, and reading print news, and we consider how pervasive the above biases are in these media, it's clear we spend a significant percentage of our waking hours unconsciously absorbing racial bias.

WHAT IS THE IMPACT OF UNCONSCIOUS RACIAL BIAS?

Over the years, researchers have documented the ways that racial bias—likely much of it unconscious—shows up in everyday interactions and leads to very real consequences for people of color.

Health

In the health industry, studies have found that doctors treat patients of color differently from white patients. In 2007, researchers administered a test of implicit bias to doctors and then asked them to make decisions about the medical treatment of a number of different patients based on reading their medical history.[22] All the sample patients in the study had symptoms indicating the patient was experiencing a heart attack. However, not all the patients got the same recommendations from the same doctor. Doctors with higher levels of measured implicit bias were less likely to recommend a lifesaving drug to black patients. On a questionnaire, these same doctors had indicated no conscious racial preferences.

Other studies showed that doctors were less likely to prescribe a cancer-preventative treatment to Latina and Chinese women than to white women and were less likely to prescribe painkillers to people of color than to white people.[23]

Safety

The stereotype that black people are violent is persistent and deeply ingrained in American thought. Researchers have found evidence of this stereotype influencing people's thoughts by making them more likely to categorize non-weapons as weapons, more likely to decide to shoot a person who is holding a weapon, and more likely to shoot a person if they are first primed with an image of a black person. Researchers point out that these associations appear to be so automatic that they are something people cannot consciously control.[24]

Stanford researcher Jennifer Eberhardt has done extensive work in this field. In one study, she showed that when people are unknowingly primed with pictures of black faces, they're more likely to identify a fuzzy picture of a gun than when they're primed with pictures of white faces. In her work with police, she sometimes tells the story of her own son internalizing the stereotype of black men as violent, even though she and her husband and children are all black.

When Eberhardt and her son boarded a plane with mostly white people, her son pointed to a black man. Despite this man's long dreadlocks being very different from his father's bald head, the boy said he looked like his dad and then said, "I hope he doesn't rob the plane." In an interview, Eberhardt described her shock at hearing her son, who was very close to his father, associate blackness and crime: "He didn't know why he said it. And he didn't know why he thought it, but at 5, you already have what you need to come to that conclusion."[25]

Racial bias is often hard to detect. One group of researchers devised a way to investigate potential racial bias in law enforcement. Researchers studied traffic stops across multiple states during daylight hours and at night. They found that during the day, police officers were more likely to stop drivers of color and were also twice as likely to search the car of the motorist if the driver was of color.[26] In the evenings, however, when there wasn't enough light for police officers to identify the race of the driver, traffic stops no longer showed the racial disparities they had during the daytime.

Employment

When people hear that the unemployment rate of black citizens is more than twice that of whites, it's easy to jump to conclusions about the job seekers themselves.[27] However, we cannot understand these numbers without also understanding the context of discriminatory hiring practices. For example, one study in Chicago showed that a vast majority of professional firms avoided recruiting in predominantly black areas of the city, opting to draw almost exclusively from white neighborhoods.[28]

In an oft-cited study, researchers sent thousands of résumés to human resource department directors.[29] They designed the résumés to have identical characteristics except for the name. Some résumés had names that most people would identify as that of a white person. Others had names people would identify with a black person. The researchers found that the human resource officers were more likely to respond to the résumé they thought was from a white person than from a black person.

Other researchers applied this same concept to candidates contacting graduate school faculty, who are the gatekeepers to the professional degrees needed to advance careers. Researchers sent identical emails of inquiry to 6,500 university professors and randomly assigned names that people would associate with someone who was black, Chinese, white, Indian, or Latino/a. Emails with white, male names got far more replies than any other group.[30]

Other studies have shown that résumés with black-identifiable names are less likely to receive interviews; blacks and Latino/a job candidates receive callbacks less often than white candidates, and well-qualified people of color get hired less often than lesser-qualified whites.[31]

Education

Stark racial disparities in test scores, suspension rates, and graduation are frequently news headlines. However, as we've seen, outcome data are not the end but the beginning of an investigation to understand what is going on. As with the data from other sectors, it's important to know the context for these racial disparities in schools.

According to a 2011 report from the National Education Policy Center, "African American students are suspended three times as often as White students—15 percent versus 5 percent. Hispanic students (7 percent) and Native American students (8 percent) are also suspended at higher rates than White students."[32] Recently, researchers at Stanford sought to shed light on racial disparities in school suspension rates. In this study, teachers were shown student discipline records with randomly assigned names. Half of the names (such as Deshawn and Darnell) suggested that the students were black, and half of the names (like Greg and Jake) suggested that the students were white.

Researchers found that teachers were more likely to assign a harsh punishment for repeated misbehavior to a student they thought was black than to a student they thought was white. They were also more likely to characterize that student as a "troublemaker" than they were a similarly misbehaving student they thought was white. In this study, teachers' perceptions of students' racial identity influenced how they chose to respond to student behavior.[33]

How might unconscious racial bias affect learning? A classic example of how unconscious bias influences the behavior of classroom teachers, leading to differing academic results among students, provides a possible answer. In this 1965 study, known as the "Pygmalion in the Classroom" experiment, researchers Rosenthal and Jacobson conducted an experiment in a public elementary school.[34] They told teachers that certain children could be expected to be "growth spurters," based on their results on a Harvard test of childhood intelligence. However, unbeknown to the teachers, the growth spurters were chosen at random, not according to their present or predicted academic capacity. A few months later, when the students were measured for academic growth after the study, the results showed the students who were randomly labeled growth spurters did, in fact, show greater intellectual development.

This study suggests that what the teachers believed to be true about students' capacity influenced their teaching and, thereby, student learning. In this case, unconscious expectation of success produced above-average outcomes. It's not a big leap to imagine that the converse is true: unconscious expectations of underperformance may produce outcomes below average.

Researchers Amanda Lewis and John Diamond provide further evidence of how unconscious bias affects learning in their book, *Despite the Best Intentions*, which describes everyday interactions at a high-performing, racially integrated Midwestern high school.[35] Through observations, interviews, and data collection, the researchers documented in detail the racially disparate ways students are treated from the amount of feedback a student gets about work to whether students are punished for violations of the dress code to whether students' can get their suspensions reduced. All of this occurred with a staff that was collectively and individually committed to racial equality.

Teachers make countless decisions that affect student learning on a daily and hourly basis. Who gets called on in class? What kind of feedback do students receive about their work? Who gets praise, and who gets redirection? Who is assigned to which teacher? How do teachers communicate with families? These decisions—which have significant ramifications for students—are all susceptible to bias. Without surfacing and addressing the impact of these biases, teachers and administrators are likely to undermine their own efforts to educate all children well.

IS THERE A SILVER BULLET?

If schools successfully identify and address unconscious racial biases, will inequities disappear? No. Schools don't operate in a vacuum. Research shows that a disproportionate number of students of color come to school already academically behind their white peers. This difference on day one isn't the result of unconscious racial bias at school. The effects of racism in our society run deep. For many of the reasons described earlier in this chapter, children of color are more likely to live in poverty, less likely to receive quality health care, and less likely to have educated parents. Young black and brown children don't get a fair start. Educators' unconscious racial bias is not responsible for all inequities.

In addition, once kids do arrive at school, addressing unconscious racial bias alone will not teach them how to read. Along with fair treatment, students need excellent teaching, a quality curriculum, high standards, and nurturing school communities. One state education leader told us, "We don't need a bleeding heart principal who talks on and on about racial bias but can't lead a school. My kids deserve better than that." We agree. For students to achieve at the highest levels, it shouldn't be too much to ask that leaders have both the expertise to carry out their job and the commitment to do it fairly.

The fact remains, unconscious racial bias lives in ourselves and our schools. Like other school leaders, we're committed to treating all students fairly. Digging deeper, past our conscious thoughts to the invisible thoughts that drive our behavior when we're not watching, we see something different. Buried in our unconscious as Americans, we believe that white students are more worthy of probing questions, second chances, and deeper learning. If we continue to probe, we'll see that while we think we're committed to treating all students equally, we act in ways that are more committed to the success of white students. We'll see we're also committed to treating black and brown students with more suspicion, more pity, more wariness, lower expectations, and lower concern. These unconscious racial biases are hard to face, and they drive more of our actions than we realize.

Regardless of the amount of effort, time, and resources education leaders put into improving the academic achievement of students of color, if unconscious racial bias is overlooked, improvement efforts may never achieve their highest potential. It may not be an exaggeration to say that if educators do not examine and counter their biases, improvement efforts will always fall short. Bias sabotages progress.

MOVING ON

While evidence of the deep-seated nature of racial bias is disturbing, we feel hopeful. There is increasing awareness in the mainstream, dominant culture of the influence of unconscious bias. The phrase "implicit bias" was used for the first time in a presidential debate, was featured in a front-page series in the *New York Times*, and is getting more attention in the research community. More and more people seek to address their biases. While deeply internalized bias is challenging to uproot, there *are* ways to reduce its negative impact. What gives us the most hope is that the clear majority of educators want the best for their students. The rest of this book describes the conditions necessary to pursue this goal and concrete steps leaders can take to make it happen.

CHAPTER 2

Start with Ourselves

It's rare to find a school leader of any racial background who talks about racial bias in his or her school. Even for those of us who entered education specifically to address racial inequities, it's rare to lead ongoing, productive discussions about racism. Most leaders we talk to feel uncomfortable about this omission but don't know what to do.

Leaders of all races tend to feel there's only one outcome from talking about race as a staff, and it's bad. The room gets tense. White teachers feel that they're accused of being racist and so shut down. Teachers of color feel frustrated and more alienated from their colleagues. Sometimes teachers respond emotionally. Other times people silently endure the meeting and then return to their work relieved in their perception that the material didn't apply to them or frustrated by their colleagues' unwillingness to consider a different perspective. Whichever response, the result is the same: no traction. People of color choose between speaking their truth or hiding their feelings in service of maintaining harmony for their colleagues. White people feel they're being told they're bad people, that they harbor ill will toward students of color, that they are intentionally producing racially disparate results. Defensiveness reigns and constructive conversation ends.

Meanwhile, there's increased distrust between teachers and the principal for either introducing the topic or leading the discussion poorly. The principal grows increasingly concerned that the staff is overly sensitive and hostile.

Things *appear* to be worse than before. Understandably, the principal vows never to do that again.

While there are many barriers to addressing the effects of racism in schools, most of them stem from one root cause. Again and again in our work with leaders—and within ourselves—we find a deep-rooted, mistaken mindset about what it means to be racist. This mindset assumes all people fit into two distinct identities: they're either racist or they're not racist. Within this mindset, these are mutually exclusive categories, mirror opposites, one good and one bad. Operating from this mindset, people are sorted into categories and judge others and themselves accordingly.

Over the years, we've seen this reductive, binary mindset in principals, teachers, and ourselves. We've seen it stifle or altogether shut down conversation and, most importantly, learning. For this reason, our first step as leaders is not to look at data or plan action steps. In order to address racism in schools, leaders first need to look within.

ADDRESS THE RACIST/NONRACIST BINARY

An African American administrator we know once bemoaned the difficulty of having frank conversations about race at a school that consisted of almost all black students and almost all white teachers. He had noticed discrepancies in the ways white and black teachers spoke to their students, and he wanted to talk about it. Yet he felt stymied in his attempts to talk about race with teachers. After multiple negative experiences, he told a colleague with exasperation, "I should just start all of our meetings by saying 'No one here is racist. Alright? I don't think any of you are racist and no one else does either.'"

We think what this administrator means is that no one here *wants* to be racist. The problem is not whether people in the room can be categorized as racist or nonracist. The crux of the problem is that educators act in racially biased ways *without realizing it*. These actions have an impact on students. If we as educators want our actions to change, we need to be able to talk about our actions objectively.

We understand the impulse behind this administrator's wish; it's a common instinct. Let's reassure everyone that this session will not make them feel accused; let's do something to prevent people from getting defensive. After all, those impulses—feeling accused and getting defensive—do prevent learning.

However, trying to allay people's fear by telling them they're not racist doesn't lead to learning either. It sends a message that people are absolved of any responsibility for examining themselves and enacting change. The need to reassure white people in particular that they're not racist is at the root of a lot of struggles to talk about race and racism in schools. We think it's important to start with the exact opposite approach.

What if the administrator had started the meeting in this way:

> Let's start by recognizing that we all have good intentions at this school. We wake up each morning wanting to do right by our students. That's one of the reasons I love working here. This meeting, however, isn't focused on how we feel about our students or what our intentions are. That's a given. Instead we're going to examine something else. We're focusing exclusively on our impact. What exactly do our students experience at our school? Despite our best intentions, we—myself included—do things unconsciously that go against our good intentions. We end up treating our students differently based on their race—and we usually don't even realize we're doing it.

We've got to move the conversation away from intentions. Most white people believe that if they have good intentions, they're all set. The logic is that our intentions drive our actions and therefore if our intentions are good, our actions will follow and will produce good results. But how can we know we are truly acting fairly? The research on unconscious bias makes it clear that our actions aren't always aligned with our intentions. When we want to understand impact, focusing on intentions is simply not relevant.

Scholars describe this pattern of associating intention with racism as central to a racist/nonracist binary: "A binary is an either/or construct that positions a social dynamic into two distinct and mutually exclusive categories. Virtually all people know how to fill in the two sides of the racism binary: if you *are* a racist, you are ignorant, bigoted, prejudiced, mean-spirited, and most likely old, Southern, and drive a pick-up truck (working-class). If you are *not* a racist, you are nice, well-intentioned, open-minded, progressive, and don't have a prejudiced bone in your body."[1] Most of us understand, at this moment in our cultural history, which is the "right" side of this binary to be on. But these categories are false, for all people hold prejudices, especially across racial lines in a society deeply divided by race.

Our experience in schools and working with school leaders has confirmed that this binary view of racism is firmly entrenched in the education sector.

Like most members of American society, most educators divide white people into two camps regarding racism. White people are either "bad white supremacist racists" or "good equality-loving nonracists." Like being judged for a crime, in this binary mindset, you're either guilty or you're innocent.

It comes as no surprise then that well-intentioned white people work very hard to make clear which side of the divide they're on to prove their innocence and to avoid what some have referred to as the "r" word or the "Scarlett R."[2] As part of this effort, white people vilify "bad white people" who are obviously racist (neo-Nazis; avowed white supremacists). And they vehemently protest (audibly or mentally) any association of themselves with racism. As author Ta-Nehisi Coates writes, "[I]n the popular vocabulary, the racist is not so much an actual person but a monster, an outcast thug who leads the lynch mob and keeps *Mein Kampf* in his back pocket."[3]

When white educators spend all their effort ducking and dodging the racist label, they miss opportunities to reduce the effects of racism on their students. People of color may be more aware of the systemic nature of racism, but they're still susceptible to the power of this racist/nonracist binary mindset. While Sarah feels the pull to prove she's one of the good white people, Tracey feels drawn into mentally condemning some people as racist and therefore irredeemable. For us as principals, this mindset led us to sort teachers into categories of good and bad, anti-racist and racist. This sorting prevented us from believing our staff could learn and grow.

RECOGNIZE THAT UNCONSCIOUS RACIAL BIAS IS . . . UNCONSCIOUS

The concept of unconscious racial bias helps decouple intentions from actions. It's an unconscious process, not a deliberate one. People aren't knowingly driving their unconscious racial bias. In some ways, focusing on unconscious racial bias is reassuring. Good intentions aren't being questioned. It's *impact* that comes under the microscope.

Recognizing that leaders harbor unconscious biases means coming face to face with the possibility—the likelihood—that they have a preference for white students and are discriminating against students of color, perhaps on a daily basis. They unconsciously nominate only white students for character awards and overlook equally qualified black students. They spend more time preparing for a meeting with white parents than on a meeting later that day with parents of color. At a quarterly data meeting, they are disappointed but not alarmed by the drop in the reading scores of two children of color. As supervisors, they don't notice that a teacher accepts sloppy work from a Latino boy in class while pushing the white girl who sits next to him to aim higher. All the while, they trust that they are doing their best to ensure students of all racial identities meet or exceed standards at school. In the monthly newsletter to families, they even write—sincerely—about the school's value of excellence for all students across all backgrounds. Most leaders, ourselves included, have unconsciously fallen into these or similar behaviors.

How can leaders hold these contradictory beliefs at the same time? To fully understand this requires breaking out of the fixed, binary mindset about identity. They have to accept that they can sincerely pursue equity and act against it at the same time. The challenge is not to distance themselves from racism but to draw closer to it, to learn how it operates in society and in themselves. For many white people, this can initially feel terrifying but ultimately can be liberating. They can shed the desperate need to prove their innocence and instead be more available to do the work of combating racism. Acknowledging that they're biased allows them to more authentically be full, flawed selves and thus be more open to reducing their potentially negative impact on black and brown students.

Leaders of all racial backgrounds benefit from examining the ways they've absorbed society's thinking about racism. They need to do this for themselves before they can help others do the same. For white people, the binary is so deeply rooted in their thinking that even after they recognize the ways unconscious bias operates, they still feel that good intentions somehow keep them immune from it. Sarah repeatedly finds herself drawn into the binary, racist/nonracist mindset. It's no longer taking her by surprise.

BEWARE THE GRIP OF THE BINARY MINDSET

Understanding this fixed, binary mindset about our racist/nonracist identity doesn't make us immune to it. As coauthors and colleagues, we observed the regular appearance of this mindset as we wrote this book. As collaborators and colleagues, we talked about the irrelevance of good intentions many times. Sarah even wrote an article titled, "Unconscious Bias: When Good Intentions

Aren't Enough."[4] On a rational level, she knows they are irrelevant. Yet the desire to feel exonerated because of good intentions continues to pull on Sarah's thinking. One example came up during one of our book meetings when we were discussing how a teacher should respond when students say, "You're racist." Sarah offered an example from her experience teaching sixth grade.

Late one spring, a teacher told Sarah that he'd overheard Mark, a recent transfer to the school, telling students in PE class that Sarah was racist. Sarah was shocked to hear this but also knew that the worst thing would be to tell this student, "No, I'm not." She knew that it's important to encourage students to speak out against injustice and particularly wanted students of color to feel empowered to speak truth to power. In this situation, however, Sarah felt confident that something else was going on. In his few days in class, it had quickly become clear that Mark's previous school had not required much work from him. He complained mightily when he had to redo work that was sloppy or incomplete and generally protested doing any schoolwork at all. Mark's comments seemed like a ten-year-old's way of saying, "I want this strict teacher to get off my back."

To address the situation, Sarah arranged to have lunch with Mark and the boys that he'd been talking to, all of whom were black. She explained what she'd heard, acknowledged that it was a possibility that she was a racist, and asked to hear whatever concerns he or the other boys had about her behavior. She explained that if she was treating them unfairly, it was important for her to hear and that if she subsequently didn't change unfair behavior, it was important that they tell a trusted adult so that something further could be done. At the time, Sarah had just read about a process for helping students of color identify whether they're being treated unfairly and how to speak up about it. She walked the boys through the four-step process and asked them to evaluate this situation accordingly.

The boys who knew Sarah said they had no concerns and then got back to laughing and joking as they finished their lunches. The new boy avoided Sarah's eyes and went along with the others, leaving Sarah satisfied that he wouldn't be using "racist" as a way of expressing his frustration toward his new teacher and the work she expected him to do.

Sarah shared this story as an example of a nondefensive teacher response to being called a racist. Tracey was alarmed. Gently but persistently, Tracey shared a different perspective: "Sarah, that boy didn't say anything directly to you. He was talking to his friends. You called him out in front of his new friends."

Tracey heard a potentially traumatizing experience for those boys, who were lectured by their white teacher about a conversation they had in private about racism. Sarah claimed not to be defensive, but in the same breath said she was confident that this was not about her behavior. Tracey asked if she'd considered that the boy might not be referring to Sarah's high expectations but instead something else. Could she really know everything about how the boy was experiencing Sarah and his new school? Could she unequivocally discount any possibility of biased behavior toward him? Finally, Tracey said to his colleague, "You acknowledge that you have unconscious biases and then you claim that you are sure you were treating this black boy fairly. Doesn't that seem . . ." Tracey hesitated and then said, "Doesn't that seem kind of arrogant?"

Tracey's response was candid and pointed, and Sarah didn't say much in the moment. Immediately after this initial conversation, however, she proceeded to go through a series of reactions that are common for white people in these interactions.

Establishing Innocence; Proving "Good White Person" Credentials

Sarah's first reaction was to assemble all the evidence she had of her innocence. She explained again the context of holding Mark to high academic standards, her success at consistently helping all of her students meet them, the extra time and support she gave Mark to ensure he would succeed. To further bolster her case, she offered evidence that the parent or guardian of each of the boys at the meeting had, at different times, thanked Sarah for being their child's favorite or most effective teacher. Surely the approval of these parents should be enough evidence to prove she was innocent.

When we're stuck in the good/bad, nonracist/racist, fixed mindset, evidence of good intentions proves that we're not racist—that we reside squarely in the nonracist category. Using this logic, any evidence that a teacher cares about children of color and has positive relationships with them or their parents absolves this teacher of any possibility of bias. This is the most obvious danger of binary thinking—positioning good intentions and biased behavior as mutually exclusive. In fact, both can be true at the same time.

Withdrawing: "This Doesn't Apply to Me"

When Tracey didn't seem moved by evidence of Sarah's good intentions, her next reaction was to withdraw. His responses were directed toward someone with racial prejudices. That did not fit her image of herself and so must not apply to her. She could listen to his concerns but feel assured that they did not involve her. She could sit this one out.

We've all seen this reaction, and many white readers have probably experienced it: withdrawing from the conversation. It's one of the great privileges of being white—they can decide the conversation doesn't pertain to them; they can choose to leave and stop thinking about it. In contrast, people of color may be able to leave the conversation, but they can't leave the issue of racism. It affects their daily experience moving through the world. Helping white people build the stamina to stay in the conversation longer is an important part of our work as leaders.

Not only do we need to keep white people engaging with the ideas longer, we also need to help them apply these ideas to themselves through critical self-examination. For example, during these conversations, Tracey recommended several video clips and short articles about whiteness for Sarah to watch and read. Sarah watched them, agreed with the author's analysis, and felt disturbed by the resistance of white people to see themselves implicated in racial bias. Then she would return to her conversation with Tracey and resist any suggestion that she might be implicated in racial bias in her interactions with Mark. She understood the ideas at a theoretical level but neglected to do the internal work of applying them to her own daily behaviors.

One of the greatest challenges in conversations with white people about racial bias is their deeply ingrained conviction that they are innocent. Even white people engaged in anti-racist work persist in this belief. They may recognize that they have absorbed unconscious racial bias, but when considering the specifics of a situation, they can't relinquish the feeling that they are one of the good white people. When we've grown up in a society that paints racists as malicious thugs, this makes sense. However, insisting on innocence precludes the hard but meaningful work of self-examination. Discovering how racial bias manifests in our interactions isn't an indictment of character. It's an opportunity to learn and grow. When white people avoid applying what they're learning about racial bias to themselves, they condemn themselves to repeat the same mistakes repeatedly, potentially hurting children and colleagues they care about.

Sorting people into the categories of either good nonracist or bad racist leads us to sort feedback into similar categories. Information about prejudiced behavior falls into the "bad racist" category and therefore doesn't pertain to us. People of all races are susceptible to this process of weeding out feedback or other information that doesn't fit their image of themselves.

Assuming We Understand

When Tracey questioned Sarah's decisions and actions, she assumed he didn't understand. It never occurred to her that maybe she was the one who didn't understand.

Here was an opportunity for Sarah to hear feedback from a person of color whose experience in school and society was distinctly different from her own. Yet rather than listen with curiosity and appreciation for him sharing this perspective, Sarah trusted her perspective and chose to ignore Tracey's. It was as if she weighed the two viewpoints equally and found her own had more merit. What this assumes, of course, is that our viewpoints are neutral. White people are so used to assuming that they see the full picture that they don't question their perspective. Ironically, this even happens when they know full well that they're biased. After all, this interaction happened while writing a book about racial bias.

As Sarah and Tracey continued to talk about their interaction, Tracey's comment about arrogance hung in the air. There was something very raw about the way he said it. Tracey's dismay at Sarah's reaction meant she had to pay attention to it eventually. At this point in their interactions, Sarah had come to recognize that when Tracey said something that felt jarring or when she was tempted to reject his comment or withdraw, she was often missing something important, something that was very clear to Tracey and just not yet clear to her. So when that jarring feeling came, Sarah was learning to recognize it as a potential blind spot.

Even though she knew the way unconscious bias operates, Sarah had refused to believe it might be influencing *her* behavior. This assumption that we see everything, this assumption that our innocence is assumed, blinds us to the ways we may cause harm. Yes, Tracey had chosen the right word, even though it was hard to hear. Assuming we can be conscious of our unconscious biases is fairly arrogant.

Acknowledging We Do Harm

One of the reasons Sarah realized she resisted Tracey's feedback so much was that she knew she loved her students. It was hard to accept the possibility that she might have acted in a way that could negatively impact them. Of all the reactions spurred by these conversations, this was where Sarah pushed back with the most resistance. She knew she had positive relationships with her students, so she couldn't wrap her head around the fact that she might simultaneously be having a negative impact. Caring and causing harm seemed incompatible.

In addition, from inside the binary mindset, Sarah interpreted Tracey's questioning as judgment, as an indictment of her character. If Tracey thought Sarah might have acted in biased ways, he must think she was an uncaring racist, a bad person. Sarah's resistance to this followed the standard playbook of interracial interactions gone wrong. She trotted out mental arguments she'd always scoffed at when other white people used them: "Why does everything have to be about race to Tracey? Couldn't this be an example where even though I'm white, I actually did the right thing? Talk about arrogant! He wasn't even there. How could he make these statements about something he had no firsthand knowledge of?"

When Sarah told a friend about her recent interactions with Tracey, the friend gently shared wise advice: "We're shaped by systems larger than ourselves in ways we're not aware of. We cause harm. We don't mean to and yet we do. All the time. It's one of the hardest things we have to come to terms with—that we love and cause harm at the same time."

This prompted a breakthrough. Once she stopped being defensive, Sarah was able to listen. She was able to acknowledge that she could act in ways that were racially ignorant or biased despite her intentions otherwise. Upon realizing this, she felt the specifics of the situation with Mark didn't really matter. Her insight was that it was possible that she caused harm. Part of our work as leaders is helping people (possibly ourselves included) live with that fact without becoming paralyzed or complacent.

Seeking to Escape the Discomfort

For white people, focused on their experience alone, this place of discomfort—of feeling falsely accused, of feeling that their intentions aren't recognized—is a hard place to stay in. During these moments, it's helpful to remember that this momentary discomfort pales in comparison to the daily experiences of discrimination most people of color experience. Yet, as was true for Sarah, many white people seek to avoid this feeling. During these interactions with Tracey, Sarah came up with countless mental arguments to allow herself to escape. She reread letters from students and their parents, recalled positive interactions with kids, recalled accolades from colleagues, and even reviewed her students' record of test scores—all to bolster the view that she was a good teacher. She thought that if she could prove that she cared about her students, then the idea that she might have caused harm couldn't be true.

Reflecting on How Biases Show Up in Conversations About Bias

At one point in the conversation, Tracey wondered if Sarah might be more open to what he was saying if a white person had said it. At first, Sarah thought this was offensive. Didn't he trust her desire to learn and grow? (There it is again—trusting that good intentions are sufficient to prevent biased behavior.) In reflecting on her resistance to some of his feedback, however, she couldn't be certain it was always from a neutral place. It was notable that the friend who helped with the breakthrough is white.

Does this mean people can't have breakthroughs across race lines? Or that they always have to retreat to their respective racial corners to gain insight? We don't think so, and we've each had enough breakthrough moments across race lines to know this can happen. At the same time, it would be foolish to think that we interact with our colleagues in a vacuum. If we have unconscious biases, they are operating all the time—with kids, with adults, and even during conversations about unconscious bias itself. So, it's incumbent upon us to regularly ask ourselves, how might my biases be playing out right now? In particular, a white person might ask: *Am I expecting to feel comfortable, to be reassured that I'm a good person, to have my viewpoint validated? Am I more skeptical of a person of color's analysis because of our society's messaging that people of color are less intellectually capable?*

There's no question Sarah consciously respects her colleague Tracey. However, these conscious thoughts and beliefs are not the issue. We can't prevent unconscious reactions, but we can try to monitor them to the best of our ability. As a reaction rises to the surface, white people can try to triangulate: *Would I have the same reaction if a white person said the same thing? How would my heart rate change in that scenario? My defensiveness? My openness and curiosity?*

Another question white leaders can ask themselves is, *Am I ready to shed this constrictive shell of defensiveness? Am I ready to stop conflating my identity with my bias?* Ultimately, the decision hinges on what leaders want for their students: teachers who prioritize their image of being good, or teachers willing to face their flaws in order to improve?

TRACEY'S EXPERIENCE WITH THESE INTERACTIONS

Tracey found this series of interactions challenging as well, although for different reasons. As Sarah went through the various emotional states described, Tracey was on the other end of the conversation. Even though this was not the first time he had had this kind of interaction with a white person, it was a draining experience. The emotional toll was probably higher precisely because it was just the latest in a long line of similar conversations. It was also hard because this was a colleague whom he respected. It was hard not to feel dismayed when even these two found themselves stuck in the same dynamic they were writing about.

The Emotional Drain

Over the years, Tracey has learned to expect resistance from white people, even close friends, when he brings up instances when they have exhibited racist or racially biased behavior. He can almost predict when it's coming. Learning the most common signs of resistance, denial, guilt, shame, and anger has aided him in developing strategies to help white friends break through their initial defensiveness and come to a place where they're able to hear and consider his feedback. These interactions, however, are emotionally taxing, not only because of the raw emotions involved but also because negative emotions are often directed at Tracey for bringing up the issue in the first place. It's easy to intellectually know it's not personal. It's harder to put that into action.

One reason people of color may not eagerly participate in conversations about race with white people is that the emotional cost can be high. Hearing Sarah talk about her interaction with Mark made Tracey think about his own experience as a student in school. Tracey was often the student who approached white teachers and even the principal with concerns about racism in school. Time after time, he'd been met with defensiveness and denial. He never encountered a teacher who wanted to understand, who wanted to hear his perspective. Sarah was not only describing marginalizing behavior that he had personally experienced as a student, but also becoming defensive in much the same ways Tracey had experienced.

For leaders of color, this is a significant occupational hazard. Choosing to engage in a conversation about possible unconscious racial bias at school means choosing to reexperience the ignorance and prejudiced behavior of a teacher with power. It can bring up examples from personal experience as well as connections to day-to-day discrimination as an adult. Because of the emotional drain, it was often hard for Tracey to concentrate on other work after these conversations.

The Invisible Labor of Teaching White People About Racism

Tracey found that teaching Sarah about her internalized racism was taxing. In preparing to work together, we had set explicit guidelines around how to share the workload, but we hadn't included the added time and burden for Tracey to continually teach and coach Sarah through her internalized racism. This intellectually and emotionally demanding work of teaching was invisible in our collaboration. Tracey was left feeling personally devalued, even though he knew what we were both experiencing was the impact of this larger oppressive system that teaches white people a distorted view of reality, including feeling certain that their view of reality is correct. Tracey could understand that the intellectual work of people of color is typically invisible and goes unrecognized by white people. He could know that this is a systemic issue, and it's not personal. Yet, it was hard to actually deal with this reality when he confronted it in our close working relationship.

While a white person may feel that conversations about race with a person of color involve an even exchange of ideas, this simply isn't the case. The person of color needs to take on the role of teacher—often repeatedly. It's heavy lifting to have to teach over and over. It's particularly heavy when white people expect you to do it. A psychiatrist isn't asked to diagnose and treat her friends or neighbors in social situations. We don't ask a carpenter to mend our broken stairs when we have him over for dinner. Yet, people of color experience this dynamic all the time.

Encouragement, Not Reassurance

In their interactions about her student, Tracey could see that Sarah wanted to be reassured of her innocence, and he didn't want to respond to these implicit requests. He knew her state of disequilibrium could yield new insights. At the same time, he was her partner and wanted to help her learn for the purpose of writing a powerful book. He also knew the power of encouragement.

So, he made a point at the end of each conversation to recognize how hard it was to have these interactions and how glad he was that we were both willing to stay in them. For example, Tracey said things like "I appreciate that we're both staying in this conversation, even when it's uncomfortable."

The white person's need for reassurance dominates and drains most conversations. It's not the responsibility of people of color to comfort white people as they learn about their role in a racist society. Developing the stamina for staying in discomfort requires effort and . . . discomfort. It's a catch-22. Intellectually, most of us understand the need to increase our tolerance for discomfort, especially in conversations about race, but when we are actually experiencing the discomfort, we are usually not thinking to ourselves, "This is great!" We are instead looking for ways to reduce the discomfort and reestablish a comfortable equilibrium. Therefore, while Tracey understood several things he could say or do to help Sarah escape her discomfort, he also knew that the best learning and growth require some level of sustained disequilibrium. Similarly, as school leaders, our work is to create the conditions for people to learn. It's what we've signed up for. We need to help people stay in that place of disequilibrium longer than they would choose to on their own.

The Feeling of Being Stuck

Tracey wasn't sure how to help Sarah get through her white defensiveness. He would see these behaviors play out before his eyes and not know how to intervene productively. He regularly tried to explain how harmful discriminatory behavior was to students. But this didn't move the conversation anywhere. Sarah would agree (somewhat impatiently—"Yes, I know. That's why I'm in education—in order to end this kind of discrimination"), but not see how that applied to this situation. Meanwhile, it seemed so obvious to Tracey. Tracey and Sarah were speaking in parallel, and Tracey couldn't figure out how to get them to meaningful interaction again.

Despite reading a great deal about whiteness and being familiar with common behaviors white people exhibit, Tracey struggled to know what to do about Sarah's resistance. Having names for different behaviors makes it clear that the resistance isn't personal. Knowing that intellectually didn't help him know what to do in live conversations. It was like witnessing someone vehemently defending their view of the world while their head is inside a brown paper bag. You're trying to explain that they may be missing some of the view—that their perspective may be missing important pieces of information.

This came most sharply into view when Tracey recommended the articles and videos for Sarah. When her behavior didn't change as a result, he assumed she hadn't read them. After all, they described the exact behaviors she was engaged in. However, she said that she had read and watched what he'd recommended. Tracey was baffled. He had spent hours scouring journals, searching video archives, and combing through book chapter after book chapter in order to help Sarah see what she was missing, but to no avail. After she'd read or watched the pieces, Sarah would simply say, "Yes, I've read the article (or watched the video) and I agree with it," but not transfer the ideas to their interactions and follow-up with, "Aha, I see why you suggested this. This explains the very blind spot you've been trying to get me to see." The connections seemed so obvious to him, and yet Sarah didn't seem to be connecting the dots.

At one point, Tracey wearily held his head in his hands. (In lighter moments, he warned that she was going to drive him to drink in the mornings.) He felt so frustrated with the process of explaining the same thing over and over. He also felt frustrated with Sarah. How could she not acknowledge that she might be wrong? How could she be so stubbornly tied to being right? Tracey was tired of her not taking responsibility for her impact—for her potential to harm and even traumatize students. Looking back, he can also see that he was stuck in the binary mindset and beginning to question her commitment to truly disrupting the racist status quo.

Compassion: An Unmerited Act of Grace

A week after the initial conversation about Mark, Tracey and Sarah got together on a Monday morning. After we both confessed to having thought about our conversation all weekend, Sarah told Tracey that she had written in her journal about it and wanted him to read her thoughts. With very little hope, he read the paragraphs she'd written defending herself. She'd listed things different parents of color had said to her, evidence of Mark's improved schoolwork later in the year, a colleague's testimony to her practice. The same old same old. We were missing each other completely. However, something was different this time when Tracey read her explanation defending herself. Something shifted when he read it. For the first time, he got an insight into what was going on in her mind, and he felt compassion for her.

Reading Sarah's reflections, he could see that she wasn't striving to deny his experience. She was trying to affirm hers. She wasn't able to see anything else. That's where we were stuck. This was about the way she saw herself. Her identity. For the first time, instead of trying to get Sarah to see her hypocrisy, to do battle with her logic, he just believed her. Something in Tracey softened as he finished reading, because when Sarah said, "Do you buy it?" he said, matter of factly, "No, I don't buy it," but this time, instead of trying to convince her, he tried to just hear her. He added genuinely, "But I believe that you sincerely believe what you are saying."

The response was pretty immediate. Sarah caught her breath when she heard Tracey acknowledge her beliefs. Something seemed to shift. Her face relaxed. She was no longer on the defensive.

After a long pause, she actually laughed out loud. It was like a blockage had been released. With relief, she said, "I get it. I'm trying to convince you I couldn't have been biased. But it's unconscious. So I can't know when I am. So even though I don't think I'm wrong, I have to be willing to see that I might not be right."

After reading her reflections, Tracey realized we had been fundamentally missing each other. He was talking about her potential impact on students, while she was talking about her intentions toward her students. Sarah saw these as connected. It was clear to Tracey they were not. Reflecting on their interaction later, Tracey realized he could have used the language of the fixed, binary mindset to help her get unstuck: "I hear you talking about intentions, but that's not what I'm talking about. I'm not questioning your intentions; I'm questioning your impact."

Tracey realized that if he views a white person's resistance as resistance to being seen as a bad person, it helps build compassion. When he can see white people's defensiveness as resistance to seeing the system they're within, it's easier to feel empathy.

The problem was that as much as Sarah couldn't see the reality of what was outside the bag, Tracey couldn't see her reality inside the bag. Going the extra mile and striving to picture her view inside that bag ended up being a key insight that prompted a breakthrough in their communication.

Mindset Affects Leadership

The challenges that surfaced in our interactions are not unique to us; they show up regularly in conversations about racism and bias. School leaders can expect the binary mindset of racist/nonracist to influence their interactions at school as well. Believing that we are either good nonracists or bad racists will challenge our ability to lead. White leaders with Sarah's perspective may get defensive when data or other feedback suggests they are biased. Like Tracey, leaders of color may feel frustrated and stymied by staff members they perceive to be irredeemable. All leaders may feel frustrated and stuck.

So how do we as educators get unstuck? The most important step is to give ourselves and our colleagues permission to be learners. As we begin trying to address racism in our schools, we need to agree to try and mess up and try again. It's no secret that talking across race about race is a minefield. Just one negative experience in this minefield or the fear of one is enough to deter even those with the strongest commitments. If we enter the work expecting to stick the landing on the very first try, we're setting ourselves up for an early exit. Tracey repeatedly tells leaders that he expects to misstep nine times out of ten in his work addressing racial bias with educators. But the tenth time results in progress, and that progress ultimately improves student learning. Are we willing to make those mistakes in the interest of making that progress?

The next step is to do what we counsel our staff and students to do when facing a daunting challenge: break it into smaller, more manageable chunks. What's one specific move we would sincerely like to make but keep putting off? What's one goal we have for ourselves in our leadership to address racism in our schools? Maybe we want to argue less and listen more in conversations. Or we'd like to be able to name race without blushing or stumbling over our words. Or we'd like to be able to speak up when we hear something racially offensive. Or we'd like to feel more patience toward staff members or colleagues who shut down or check out during these conversations.

After identifying a specific skill to improve, we've found it helpful to apply the concept of "competing commitments" to shed light on why we're stuck. This concept, from psychologists Robert Kegan and Lisa Lahey, explains that when we urgently want to improve at something, we often have an even stronger commitment inside us that prevents us from making the change.[5]

This is the root cause of the problem. This is what's preventing us from taking the action we want to take. As we've coached principals and reflected on our own stuck points related to conversations about race and racism, we've realized that when we trace the challenge back to its roots, we almost always bump up against this binary mindset defining ourselves and others as either racists or not racists. Most of us harbor a deep-seated commitment to end up on the good side of the binary. Thus, the reason we're stuck is that we're not allowing ourselves or others to be learners on a developmental continuum of learning. And if mistakes aren't possible, progress isn't either.

The two of us are striving to replace the binary mindset with a developmental perspective. We see ourselves and others on a continuous journey to become increasingly aware of the way racism operates in our society and influences our day-to-day thinking. It's an ongoing process of growth. As commentator Jay Smooth says, it's not like getting your tonsils out—"I'm not racist, I had that removed three years ago." Rather it's more like daily dental hygiene. Cleaning off the gunk that accumulates every day is just part of our regular routine.[6]

However, the binary mindset is deeply rooted in our psyche. So we find that we need to continually examine our thinking to find when we're stuck in that mindset and to replace it with a growth mindset.

SET IMPROVEMENT GOALS AND EXAMINE COMPETING COMMITMENTS

We've each identified specific areas for improvement. For example, Tracey has committed his career to helping educators grow in their understanding of race and racism in education. However, he realized that he was not having productive conversations with white people after they said something he perceived to be racist. As the person continued to speak, Tracey would mentally assemble an arsenal of counterpoints and/or ways to entrap the person in a contradiction or inconsistency. He also found himself skeptical that the person truly cared about students of color. Not surprisingly, his approach wasn't leading educators to grow. When Tracey was honest with himself, however, he could recognize that these exchanges felt personally satisfying. Condemning the other person's beliefs and intentions affirmed Tracey's righteous, antiracist stance, and the cycle would repeat. Thus, the stuck point.

After deep reflection on why his commitment to changing mindsets wasn't getting traction, Tracey recognized the racist/nonracist binary mindset was shaping his thinking. As long as he kept establishing himself and the other person as on opposite sides of the binary, no new strategy or questioning technique was going to change these interactions. Tracey committed to addressing that root cause and disrupting his binary mindset about others and himself.

Tracey is now actively committed to disrupting this mindset, for himself and others. Rather than divide people into categories of bad racist, good nonracist, Tracey seeks to see others and himself on a continuum of learning about their own racial identities. While previously he was only able to see himself as an authority, now he's more willing to see himself as a learner. While previously he assumed that racist beliefs come from a place of malice, he now realizes that's not always true and he's able to feel genuine empathy for those whose statements sound racist but are still learners like himself.

Sarah set a personal improvement goal to be able to name her unconscious racial bias publicly. If she could model this step, she knew she would make it easier for others to enter into the conversation and own their unconscious biases as well. However, she first had to confront her fear that standing in front of people and acknowledging that she was biased would paint her as a cross-burning racist whom no one could trust. She had to confront her desire to protect her identity as one of the "good white people."

She committed to testing out small steps: "If I share my bias with this group, will it diminish my ability to work with people of color? Will they trust me less? Will white people stop listening to my perspective because they are repelled by what I've revealed?" What she's learned is that one of the most productive ways for her to learn about race and racism is to acknowledge her blind spots up front, which opens the door to learning. Students and colleagues tell her they appreciate her honesty and sometimes alert her to another blind spot she hadn't noticed, another way she's lost sight of her privilege.

We've each made progress on our individual improvement goals. Tracey is able to suspend judgment for longer periods of time during discussions of race and increasingly is able to feel fellowship with other learners of all races committed to addressing racism. Sarah talks about her biases more publicly and less frequently finds herself defending her identity as the good white person. This progress encourages us to continue working on these improvement goals and to create new ones. As with most self-improvement efforts, each step of progress reveals more layers of progress to be made.

With a topic as complex as racism, it's no surprise the human mind has come up with all sorts of escape hatches to avoid dealing with the challenge. The binary mindset that sorts people into racists/nonracists is one of the most damaging. When we sort others and ourselves into simplistic categories of bad and good, we're deceiving ourselves. When we face the complex reality that racial bias influences all of us, we begin to shed fear and shame and can help others do the same. Then we can link arms and do the work of creating communities where students, and not fragile egos, come first.

CHAPTER 3

Normalize Talking About Race and Bias

In schools tackling bias, adults and students talk about race regularly. Teachers in the library after school ask about books with black and brown protagonists. Members of a seventh-grade team examining math data wonder aloud about students on the intervention list: "We haven't been able to move this group of black girls off the list, and my interventions are not working. Help me understand what's going on here. What am I missing?" A student teacher talks to his mentor about how to lead a discussion of a racially charged event in the reading assignment. Two teachers at the copy machine ask whether the black boys in their classes are unfairly being singled out at dismissal time and decide to investigate the issue. In order for schools to investigate where racial bias lives in their practice, people first need to be able to simply name race. Leaders play an important role.

What leaders say and pay attention to gets noticed. Equally important, however, are the topics we as leaders ignore, the issues around which we remain publicly silent. If we're silent about race, our community is likely to be silent as well. How do we create a whole-school community where talking about race and racial bias is not sidestepped or siloed but approached head-on, regularly?

Most white people don't talk about race at all. And while people of color have likely talked about race for most of their lives, few talk about race in racially heterogeneous environments. So most of us—of all races—suffer from a lack of experience. This can make efforts awkward and uncomfortable, so we return to not talking about race much.

In order to talk about racial bias, faculty need to be able to talk collaboratively about race—their own and others'—in ways that are constructive, curious, honest, and open. A good dash of humility and self-deprecating humor helps as well. School communities have to get to a place where talking about race and racial bias isn't an event. It doesn't only happen on a designated professional development day. Instead, it simply becomes the way we talk in our schools. It becomes *normal*.

Despite a commitment to leading for racial equity, when the two of us first became school principals, neither of us directly addressed racial bias. On the contrary, we both deliberately avoided such conversations with the whole staff. We each had reasons.

Before becoming a principal, Tracey tried the direct approach. At one meeting, when he was an assistant principal at a middle school, he presented data showing that black students were getting suspended for the same behaviors that white students were engaging in without getting suspended. He pointed out what seemed obvious to him: the school was treating students of color differently from white students. Things got uncomfortable pretty quickly: "I treat all students the same! I'm not racist. I don't see color. These kids need to learn how to behave." "I talk to white students and they stop, but I just can't get through to the black students. Are you accusing us of being racist?" As a result of this meeting, most teachers were less open to Tracey's feedback and certainly not inclined to take responsibility for disparate outcomes in student data.

Because of this meeting and the fallout he experienced from it, Tracey decided to take a different approach when he became the principal of a high school. To prevent what he saw as white teachers' inevitable defensiveness, he would not name race. Instead he talked about "underperforming groups" or "kids not represented in the AP classes." He talked one-on-one with teachers about individual students rather than talk to the whole staff overtly about racial disparities in the data.

Sarah's experience was different, but it led to the same outcome when she became a principal. When she was a teacher, she co-led an anti-racism, anti-bias parent-teacher discussion group. Parents and teachers of all races showed up regularly to these evening meetings to discuss an article or some scenarios or a question regarding race. It was a volunteer group with participation varying from twenty to forty people. At the meetings, conversations were intense and rarely wrapped up neatly. Typically, something volatile came up;

conversations raised a host of emotions from confusion to compassion to frustration. No matter what their emotions during the meeting, most people left feeling emotionally exhausted. Notably though, both white people and people of color kept coming. The people who attended said it was important work and they were glad it was happening.

Despite this positive feedback, when Sarah became a principal, she chose not to lead these same conversations with her staff. She found it nerve-wracking to consider planning and leading these meetings without the help of two women of color who had been co-leaders of the parent-teacher group. The fallout seemed potentially more risky. She wasn't confident she would be able to handle the messiness of the conversations, especially in a mandatory group rather than the previous voluntary group. Instead, she decided that focusing on data would be a less complicated way to achieve the same goals. She believed the staff could talk about ways to improve the academic achievement of students of color without talking about race. She still talked to individual teachers about race and potential bias, but in those first years of her principalship, it wasn't on the staff meeting calendar, in the school improvement plan, or part of the official staff conversation.

The fact that our two approaches as new principals somewhat mirrored each other at first surprised us. Then, after reflection, it seemed perfectly logical and in line with what we have seen in other schools around the country.

LEADERS CONFRONT MULTIPLE MINEFIELDS

For both white leaders and leaders of color, talking about race can feel like walking through a minefield. It's no wonder most of us avoid it. Some of our fears are the same. What do I say when things go "wrong"? When someone says something offensive, how should I respond? As the leader, how do I keep the conversation open so that everyone feels safe to speak honestly? But if people speak honestly and say something offensive, then what? What do I say and do? Will people shut down because they feel I've accused them of being racist? Will the word spread around the district that my leadership approach is to throw accusations around? Alternatively, will people hear how I garbled my response to someone and see me as incompetent?

Especially for new principals who haven't gotten to know their teachers, how will these conversations affect relationships with the faculty? And their relationships with each other? Leaders know how important trust is within a school community. What if conversations about race undermine mutual trust? What if the damage is irreparable? With all that school leaders have to tackle, the risk of potentially sabotaging staff trust seems untenable.

In addition, a common fear among leaders of color is that white teachers will assume they're pushing a personal agenda. Teachers will think that the only thing they care about is bringing up the race card and that everything they say will be explicitly or implicitly about race. Before they start to speak, staff members will either dismiss what they have to say or become defensive.

One new administrator told us, "As a leader of color, I'm worried that if I constantly bring up the way people are biased, they're going to stop being receptive. I'm constantly asking myself whether I want to be branded—'Oh, he only thinks about diversity'—and then people stop listening to me." This leader worked at a charter school where his contract was up for renewal each year. He explained the complex dance he had to perform in his work:

> I have to play politics so that I can get to the place where I can do the work, knowing they can get rid of me at any point. It's a delicate balance—you've got to appease your staff of color who are demanding that their colleagues get a better awareness of the kids they're serving. And you've got to balance that with the people who came to teach and didn't come to talk about race. They don't want to be told they're being racist and biased. But the problem is, they are being racist and biased.

To add to the challenge, many leaders of color find themselves witnessing or listening to teachers saying and doing the very things that were exclusionary and offensive to them as students when they were in grade school. Tracey experienced this in the conversations with Sarah about her student, described in chapter 2. One leader of color described this experience to us as re-traumatizing: "I have to invite teachers' honest thoughts and questions. When they start saying things that are biased, I know it doesn't help to shut them down. I know I have to be a good listener. At the same time, I'm standing there reliving the trauma I experienced in high school when teachers didn't see my full potential. It takes a lot of strength to lead this work as a person of color." If some leaders of color look weary, it's because this work can feel like pushing back the tide.

With so much apprehension about talking about race, it's not surprising that many leaders avoid it. At the same time, if we avoid talking about race, how can we expect to get past the uneasiness? Meanwhile, back at both of our schools, the problem persisted. While each school included self-aware teachers committed to examining their own biases, there were other teachers who needed help. We were both deeply committed to ending racial disparities in student learning at our schools. We also both felt an uneasy suspicion that something might be missing in our approach.

We came to realize that missing piece was a developmental, skill-building approach. Rather than push everyone into the deep end right away, we needed to know our staff and their knowledge, experience, and skill in talking about race. As any teacher would do with students, we could then use this information to create the conditions and preparation necessary for productive learning to occur.

In their book, *The Guide for White Women Who Teach Black Boys*, the authors reference a conversation with Howard Stevenson, a professor of psychology, who points out a critical perspective for leaders to hold.[1] Stevenson cautions that when we view people's anxiety or inability to talk productively about race as a matter of character, it stifles our ability to address it. Instead, we need to view these behaviors as simply a sign that the teacher needs skill building. As the authors explain further, when you struggle to talk about race, "It is a sign you may lack the skills and competencies to engage in the conversation. It means you need to acquire a skill set you do not currently have—*but it is one you can gain.* [our emphasis] In fact, it is one all educators must have."[2] We need to beware of the binary mindset that would immediately judge and characterize people as racist and irredeemable when they avoid race or stumble over their words.

Breaking Out of the "Colorblind" Illusion

A common minefield is when well-intentioned educators strive to be "colorblind." They say that they don't consider or pay attention to the race of anyone they interact with or hear about. Within this line of thinking, to be aware of someone's race is to treat them differently and thus be racist. People who claim to be colorblind think that the way to increase equity is by not acknowledging differences.

The strategy of colorblindness may be well intentioned, but it's not helpful. On the contrary, it's problematic for many reasons. Differences aren't something to be feared. Would we say that we don't see hair color? Why do people feel they shouldn't see skin color? We can't build the trust needed to do hard work together without recognizing and valuing people's full selves.

Furthermore, our society is most certainly *not* colorblind. The sampling of studies from chapter 1 demonstrates that we live in a society where people are treated differently based on race, whether consciously or unconsciously. Ignoring these facts doesn't make them go away. As diversity and inclusion expert Verna Myers says, if we want to address the negative ways our society views people of color, we need to "walk boldly towards them."[3] Putting on blindfolds doesn't help us do that.

Perhaps one of the most damaging aspects of colorblindness, however, is that it prevents white people from seeing their whiteness and the privilege that comes with it. Unlike people of color, most white people can go through the day not consciously aware of their racialized experience because they don't personally experience racism. As leaders, we need to understand the profound impact of this lack of consciousness. It may be the central reason so many white teachers (and some white leaders) aren't comfortable talking about race. They don't see how it applies to them.

As philosopher José Medina explains, colorblindness "requires being actively and proudly ignorant of social positionality, which involves a double epistemic failure: a failure in self-knowledge and a failure in the knowledge of others with whom one is intimately related."[4] We recognize the irony in explaining earlier in this book that race is a social construct that has no biological foundation and now in emphasizing the importance of naming and seeing race. As Medina points out, we as leaders need to focus on race because of the power it holds in our society—the positionality it lends. The lie constructed hundreds of years ago to describe the concept of "race" hasn't yet been deconstructed. Being colorblind won't make it go away.

Is Your School Colormute?

A by-product of being colorblind is being colormute. Conversations tend to skirt around race. We've heard white teachers refer to "multicultural kids," "urban kids," "diverse kids," "ethnic kids," and "these kids." Children themselves aren't multicultural or diverse, although an overall community might be, and by definition we all have an ethnicity. "Urban" and "these kids" are generally accepted to mean "black" and "brown" students, which educators tend to avoid saying.

Even when schools are required to set goals and write improvement plans to "raise the achievement of our Latino students by 10 percentage points" or "decrease the number of out-of-school suspensions of our African American students," few schools go beyond these statements to actually talk about race. Individual teachers may have conversations in the parking lot or behind closed doors, but in staff meetings, team time, and other official settings, talking about race is considered risky territory and just not done. Researcher Mica Pollock coined the term "colormute" to describe the phenomenon of educators avoiding talking about race in schools.[5] According to her research, not only do we not talk *about* race in schools, too often we don't even *name* race.

Conversations about race *are* happening among students, however. Whether in a kindergarten classroom ("How come his skin is so dark?") or a high school classroom ("The black kids own the football and basketball teams, but the white kids rule soccer and hockey"), kids have questions, observations, and a natural curiosity to talk about race. Educators need to know how to respond. Teachers need to be able to navigate conversations about everything from physical differences to police shootings to internment camps and why we have Black History Month. How do we want those conversations to go? What do we want the culture to be in talking about race at our school?

Often, students see the problem with a colormute approach more clearly than adults. The white daughter of a friend of ours described an incident that happened during her first week of middle school. Students at Erin's suburban school gathered outside waiting for the morning bell to ring so they could enter the building. As a group of white students approached a group of black students, one of the white students called a black student the N-word. The black student responded by hitting the white student. As the two groups of students grew into a much bigger crowd, adults rushed to intervene, took the two students away, and sent the rest of the students into the building.

What was the school's response after this? Not a single teacher spoke to students about it, and the principal sent an email to families saying that there had been "an incident" at school that morning and that the school was taking care of it. No mention of the racial epithet or the racially charged situation so many students witnessed. Just an incident, nothing more.

At home, Erin confirmed what most educators could predict: kids talked about the incident nonstop at lunch, after school, and on social media. Without adult guidance, they processed it themselves, and at least some knew they were missing something. "Teachers didn't talk about it with us at all," Erin said with indignation. She resented feeling unprepared and uncomfortable discussing race at school. She said with dismay, "I even felt bad when I was just telling you what happened—like it was bad to say that the kid was black. Like that was a bad thing!" This teenager could sense she was being denied something—in this case, proficiency in talking about race—and she was angry. She realized her teachers' colormute response was inhibiting her own learning, and she discovered she was unconsciously internalizing this taboo.

Erin's principal let her community down and paved the way for increased rather than decreased racial tension at her school. Erin and other students at her school wanted to be able to talk and think about the racial tension at school in a constructive way, and they needed help. No doubt parents in the community and even teachers in the school needed help as well. The school needed a leader willing to name race.

Why is naming race—or even naming racial differences like skin color—so taboo for white people? Shannon Sullivan, the author of *Good White People: The Problem with Middle-Class White Anti-Racism*, offers one reason.[6] In this country, the people who have a monopoly on using race labels are white supremacists. For most white people, when they picture a white person talking about race, they picture someone spewing hatred. There aren't a lot of other role models. Thus, for many white people, talking about race has become synonymous with being racist. As in the middle school incident, we see this played out over and over in schools.

One day when Sarah was a principal, she overheard an exchange in the hallway between a student and a substitute teacher. The young student asked a question about a school volunteer, "Is she Chinese?" The teacher quickly shushed him and said sternly, "Don't say that. That's not nice." In this case, Chinese is a nationality, not a race label, but for many non-Asian students, it's the label they use for Asian or Asian American. This child seemed to be wondering in general about racial categories and didn't have the language to know what to ask. In the teacher's shushing response, she communicated clearly not only that racial categories are something to avoid, but that talking about them is mean.

Sarah later followed up with the student to say simply that she knew his question wasn't mean, that the volunteer he asked about was born in the United States and so is American, but that she looks like people who come from countries in East Asia. Maybe her parents or grandparents or other family members were born in one of those countries and moved here. The student seemed satisfied with the clarification.

Why didn't Sarah follow up with the teacher? It should have been simple enough to use the same straightforward approach she'd taken with the student: "I heard your exchange and wondered what made you say his question was mean" or "I'm concerned that your response tells students we can't talk about race at our school. Is that your intention?" Yet Sarah didn't take either of these approaches and did not engage in a conversation with the adult about race.

Stuck in her racist/nonracist mindset, Sarah had mentally sorted this woman into the bad side of the binary. In this context, giving feedback would simply be telling the woman she was a bad person, which didn't feel productive. While Sarah didn't shy away from having difficult conversations about teaching practice and professional habits, this felt different. This felt like critiquing the woman's character. Instead, she made a mental note to take the woman off the list of substitute teachers and moved on. It could have been an opportunity to help this woman learn skills she did not have: how to talk about race with children, how to think about race herself, how to reflect on her racial identity, and how that shapes her perspective. She didn't get that opportunity to learn because Sarah didn't see these as teachable skills and so didn't take responsibility to teach them.

Tracey had similar examples of hearing something offensive and putting the teacher in the "doesn't get it, how can I minimize their damage" category. In other words, both of us have engaged in colormute behavior. As leaders, as long as we view teachers as "bad" or ill-intentioned, we have very little chance of changing practice. With reflection, we might also acknowledge that this view gives us an easy out. We can avoid facing our own incompetence in this follow-up conversation and preserve our personal sense of righteousness: *We aren't like that person; we're on the good side of the binary.* In so doing, we deprive ourselves and our staff of learning. We also miss opportunities to diminish the impact of racial bias in our school community.

NAME RACE

An experience from a high school drawing class serves as a vivid metaphor for the importance of teaching white teachers to name race.[7] While learning to draw, the class of all-white students faced a new situation. The live model that day was African American, unlike all the previous models, who had been white. As the teacher, who was visiting from France, walked around the classroom watching the students sketch, he grew more and more baffled. None of the students were depicting the model's skin color. He finally told the students to gather around, and he drew the model with shading to show her dark skin. He showed students how to make her skin color visible in their drawings and then directed them to go back to their easels and do the same. As leaders, we can help people see that they don't need to be afraid of shading in the picture. We can teach them how to do it.

When describing a student or someone else at school, many people will behave like these art students. They'll tell everything about the child except skin color. Wouldn't that additional piece of information help us quickly and easily picture the child in question? When describing anyone, Sarah noticed as a principal that many white people found it disconcerting when she included race as a normal descriptor like hair color or height.

She initially named race only for people of color, until she realized that doing so reinforced the status quo that white is "normal" and everything else is "other." So she started naming race for white people as well: "You can find the fourth-grade teacher in the cafeteria this period. She's tall, white, has long brown hair in a ponytail." "Can you give this to Evan? He's the small, black kid with the backpack standing outside the office right now." "Do you know Susan's mom? She's white, blond hair, usually hangs out with her son in the park after school." For many white people, just this act of including race in descriptions of people is a first step toward normalizing racial differences.

Race is clearly relevant when describing someone's appearance, but what about other times in conversation? Sometimes we don't need to know the race of a person to understand the situation. Other times we do. Noticing the patterns of when we use racialized language and when we avoid it is helpful.

Are we more comfortable using race labels when they are in line with popular stereotypes: "This big black guy . . .," "The Mexican cleaning lady . . ."? Does racial language appear more often when we talk about misbehavior than when we talk about success? Do we omit racial language in situations involving white people, where we would be inclined to include a racial identifier if the person were of color?

When describing the kids who were playing together at recess, is it important to say they were all black? What about when describing the group of mothers who chat in the lobby each day after school starts? Or the father who was upset that his child missed the bus home? Is race relevant to the story? And when we're making class assignments, should we attend to race? Whether or not we name race in these situations reflects whether we think it has bearing on the situation. And this, in turn, reflects the range of associations we have with race. We learn a lot about ourselves by observing our own inclinations and those of others and analyzing what unknown biases may be behind them.

One colleague of ours, a white education leader, described her effort to grow more comfortable naming race. Initially, she noticed that whenever she talked about race, she had a physical reaction of her heart racing and her speech getting faster. She recognized that this was a product of society's stigma and interfered with her ability to address racial inequities in schools. She made a commitment to practice talking about race with friends and family until she could name race labels and not break out in a sweat. She practiced until it felt normal.[8]

Sarah grew up regularly talking about race with her family, yet she experiences a heightened awareness using race terms with people she doesn't know. Across contexts, white people use race terms in a variety of ways, often negative. So after speaking, the race labels seem to hang in the air a few moments longer for Sarah as she wonders how this particular white listener will interpret them. She can feel herself want to be sure the listener identifies her on the right side of the racist/nonracist binary. She finds herself wondering, "Should I throw in a few clarifying statements to ensure nothing is misunderstood, to distinguish myself from the white people who use race labels in a derogatory way?" Like it or not, race labels spoken by white people in our society can feel like loaded terms. This makes it all the more important to normalize talking about race.

Even if a leader doesn't get sweaty and nervous talking about race, addressing this phenomenon is something all leaders need to think about. Leaders work with teachers who have different levels of comfort naming and talking about race. We can't assume everyone will be as motivated or persistent as our colleague who deliberately practiced with friends and family, especially since we know it's hard to practice something we find uncomfortable. For this reason, leaders need to create the conditions for staff to practice talking about race.

Create Space to Talk About Racialized Experiences

For leaders who aren't experienced talking about race in mixed-race contexts, the first step is to practice. Then leaders are better equipped to help their faculty gain skills in talking about race regularly. Here's where a developmental rather than binary view of the relationship to racism helps a great deal. If we believe that we're all learners striving to filter out the smog of racism, we'll believe that we can improve our own and others' ability to talk about race.

One place to start this practice is with individuals' own life experiences. What early memory do you have of talking about race? Who is a person of your race whom you look to as a model of anti-racism and what does that person do that you respect? What is a favorite movie or book that represents your racialized experience well? Logging time in these kinds of conversations provides needed practice and some early wins ("See? We were able to talk about race and the staff didn't turn on each other! We even learned important things about our colleagues"). Building this foundation allows us to subsequently move into more high-risk conversations, analysis, and reflection.

For many white educators who feel they are colorblind, transitioning to talking about race requires that they first recognize that they *have* a racialized perspective. Here lies one of the great racial divides in our country. Most people of color understand from an early age that their personal experience is influenced by race. White people don't understand. White people typically don't grow up conscious of how invisible but consequential racial hierarchies influence their life. As a result, it's likely that most white educators won't have experience thinking about their whiteness, let alone talking about it. They need prompting. Helping white educators see how race has shaped—and continues to influence—their life experience is a critical first step in what psychologists call racial identity development.[9]

Racial identity development isn't just for white people. A school leader in Detroit shared a wake-up moment for him. At the end of each staff meeting, he had been showing his faculty short video clips to build a shared understanding of deeper learning. After about ten videos, a teacher came up to him after the meeting and said, "Could one of your examples of excellent teaching show a teacher of color?" This school leader was taken aback. He hadn't noticed that all of the model teachers were white. This teacher and most of her colleagues were black. So was the school leader. Reflecting on this, he said, "Shame on me for not even noticing. I was so glad when this teacher pointed it out to me. It's an awareness I need to have."

A school in Washington, DC, has made a commitment to racial identity development as part of its collaborative work. Capital City Public Charter School (CCPCS) enrolls almost a thousand students from every ward in Washington, DC, on its K–12 campus. The school enrolls primarily students of color, with 30 percent African American, 57 percent Latino/a, 7 percent white, 2 percent Asian, and 4 percent other racial identifier. Eighteen percent of the students are English language learners. The school is classified as a Title I school, with 72 percent of students coming from low-income families. Since graduating its first class in 2012, 100 percent of the school's seniors have been accepted to college.

For years, CCPCS hired outside consultants to lead various training sessions about addressing racism in school. For years, it felt useful but dissatisfying, like a token effort. Whole-staff conversations happened only a few times a year and didn't seem integrated into year-round conversations. School leaders wanted to normalize talking about race and racial identity throughout their work. To support this effort, they sent a core group of staff members for training to lead conversations about race and racism. Members of this group formed the Equity Core Committee, which designs ongoing professional learning for staff about race. Now, leaders reserve time approximately every six weeks for staff in all roles across the school to engage in equity work together. The work takes many forms, but staff regularly meet in small groups of about ten to twelve called Equity Learning Communities. They may examine a common text, which might be a question, video, article, or artwork or investigate a dilemma of practice. Following designated protocols, staff take turns sharing personal responses, experiences, and reflections about the prompt, which focuses on racial identity.

Importantly, the sessions do not initially include advice about lesson planning, suggestions of resources to use with students, or any specific focus on classroom teaching. A guidance document suggests that facilitators use the following introduction:

> We know that a lot of people come into the work wanting ideas that they can use in their classroom right away. That is not what we will get to today. The work needs to begin with looking at ourselves—what we bring to our work ("the skin I'm in") and the historical and societal influences. It also needs to focus on building a strong community where we can have courageous conversations. The focus is on giving you the tools and skills to be leaders for equity.

White people, in particular, can feel uncomfortable staying in the conversation about the experience of being white. It's not something white people are used to consciously thinking about. Schools trying this approach can expect confusion, at least, and most likely some frustration and resistance as well. Leaders at Capital City say that while most staff members report the sessions are helpful, there are always a few teachers who don't see the value of the meetings. In every session, at least a few write on the evaluation form some variation of "I wish I could just get some practical ideas for what to do in the classroom." Capital City leaders certainly want to support teachers with practical ideas. This meeting, however, has a different purpose. The leaders hold firm in their conviction that these meetings serve an important function. Teachers of all racial backgrounds need support in their racial identity development in order to effectively reach across differences in their teaching. Head of School Karen Dresden explains the purpose of these meetings this way:

> The skills you need are about how to respond to ad hoc situations in your classroom, stuff that you can't lesson plan for. So we need to build your judgment, your overall capacity to understand issues around race so you're better equipped for those situations. We also need to give you time and practice to figure out the right language to use with kids—for example, how to talk about prejudice with kindergarteners versus ninth graders, how to normalize talking about race and racism in your classroom. Separate from all of this, we also need to give you tools and practice to lead lessons about this, but that's a different skill. That's something you can plan for. What we're building capacity for is the stuff you can't plan for: our own internal reactions and responses.[10]

As a teacher facilitator of this work explained, "The work of the Equity Core Committee is helping teachers tell their story so they can help students tell their story . . . Unlike learning to teach a particular math or reading skill, you don't ever become the perfect expert at this training. It's a journey and no one is ever the perfect teacher who has no bias, everyone is on the journey."

Learn About Racial Identity

How do you teach about racial identity? A colleague of ours starts workshops by having people write and share a racial autobiography with colleagues. In our work with school leaders, we've led a similar process using a protocol called the "River of Life" that invites participants to illustrate their racial autobiography as a river with different experiences showing up as twists, turns, waterfalls, shallows, and so on along the way. As participants describe their racialized experiences (and for some people, as they practice talking about race for the first time), they learn details about each other's lives and gain insights into their own. For facilitators designing learning sessions, we've seen the following learning target capture this goal: "I can examine my personal narrative around my racial identity to notice its impact on and implications for my work as an educator."[11] As people hear from others and reflect deeply on their own experiences, they grow their racial consciousness.

The author of *Courageous Conversations About Race*, Glenn Singleton, describes a "racial consciousness flow chart," which begins with "I don't know I don't know" and "I don't know but I think I do." The goal is to move out of these stages to "I know I don't know" and finally "I know I know."[12] Singleton then prompts readers to "[t]hink of an experience when your racial consciousness was developed. Name and reflect on the discovery, then trace it through the stages outlined previously." We've seen facilitators use the flow chart and this prompt to develop people's racial consciousness as well.

The following are some other initial prompts for a faculty to talk about race together:

- "Tell about your earliest memory of race."
- "What does discrimination feel like?"
- "What does racial empowerment look like for you?"
- "How are you impacted by [an event in the news regarding race]? If you haven't been impacted, why do you think this is the case?"[13]

In all of these examples, the structure favors the personal over the theoretical. Former codirector of the National SEED Project on Inclusive Curriculum (Seeking Educational Equity and Diversity) Emily Style encourages us to value the "scholarship in the selves" not just the "scholarship on the shelves."[14]

What about schools where there isn't racial diversity among staff members? Focusing on racialized experiences is still a valuable exercise. White people don't have a uniform experience of how they've experienced their whiteness. However, a crucial way for white people to learn about their own racial identity is to hear how people of color experience racism in their daily lives. Educator Sonia Nieto requires her mostly white education students to read coming-of-age stories from students of all different racial backgrounds. There are also many videos online of people of color and white people talking about their racial identity.

As important as it is for white educators to learn about how people of color experience racism, it is also useful for people of color to learn how white people relate to race and racism. Silence from white people does not contribute to the collective understanding. While most people of color typically have experience talking and thinking about race, they may not have had conversations about race with white people, especially those who do not understand the concept of racism. For this reason, it's valuable for white people to share their honest experience and reactions. Rather than sit silently, a white person can say, "I realize I don't think about race much" or "I don't understand why race is so important." In a racially heterogeneous group, this honest sharing and perspective are vital to cross-racial understanding and helping people of color learn about the white perspective of their colleagues.

At one school with a majority white staff working with a majority black student body, the principal found online video interviews of black students talking about their experiences in high school. After watching them at a staff meeting, teachers asked to see more. This led administrators to survey, interview, and videotape black students in their own school to share with teachers. When a student well known and beloved by many teachers said she felt the school's environment was racially hostile, many teachers were shocked. While some teachers dismissed it as a teenager parroting what was trendy in the news, others considered for the first time that they might have blind spots and needed to learn more about them.

Outside perspectives can be valuable, but the focus of work remains on ourselves. Learning about racial identity requires us to dig deep. Conversation structures help us do this.

Use Protocols and Other Conversation Structures to Talk About Race

At one urban middle school, the principal has long prioritized helping his staff understand their racial identities in order to be more effective teachers. As at Capital City, administrators schedule time for the staff to discuss race and racism. However, for several years, staff gave mixed reviews of the meetings. People described the meetings as often aimless discussions where some people would pontificate and others would endure. The quality of the meetings depended largely on who was in the group and the skill of the group leader. Then the school adopted a new structure for the meetings. As with Capital City, a central committee selected a common text and protocol that team leaders used to facilitate the meetings. According to one longtime teacher, it was like night and day. There was a sense of purpose. Rather than a meandering conversation, the goal became clearer: to deliberately hear different perspectives. Not to debate them, not to come up with the just-right refute. But to listen to each other respond to the same prompt and hear the differences in the room.

A conversation protocol does not have to be complicated. The purpose is to provide simple structures so people know what is expected of them, so everyone participates, so no one dominates, and often to ensure a deep analysis from multiple perspectives.

In their thirty years of work with educators, facilitators with SEED have facilitated groups of educators in conversations about power and privilege, including addressing racism. SEED founder Peggy McIntosh uses an exercise that she and colleague Victor Lewis devised called "serial testimony," in which the facilitator asks a question that prompts a brief answer. For example, *"What is a key experience that shaped the way you see and understand race?" "Tell about a time you had a courageous conversation about race or a time when you wish you had spoken up but didn't"* or *"Who were you taught to look down upon when you were growing up? Who were you taught to look up to?"* After people have a moment to reflect and possibly journal about their thoughts, each person has one minute (in smaller groups, sometimes two) to respond to the prompt. (Another structured conversation—called the microlab protocol—is similar but works in groups of three so sharing time can be longer.)

As anyone who has used conversation structures knows, it's critical to use a timer (an egg timer, a phone with a gentle alarm, or a chime) and insist that participants follow it. During serial testimony, each person's time is his or hers alone. No one may respond to the sharing before, during, or after; no cross-talk is allowed. The goal is simply to allow each person to share a perspective or experience without evaluation, judgment, or debate.

Why do some protocols and the serial testimony exercise stipulate that there is no sharing about what other people have said? Too often, people's words are questioned, doubted, or compared to someone else's experience. The purpose of these structures is to surface and value each person's experience equally. People may be more likely to share their experience if they know the group will hear it but not dissect it.

For many white people, the words and reflections feel awkward and unfamiliar if this is their first time thinking about their racialized experience. People may seek more comfortable conversational territory, such as responding to what someone else said and thus avoiding introspection. While conversation structures are often seen as tools to prevent a few people from dominating the conversation, they can also be a means of ensuring that everyone has to reflect.

Not all conversation structures discourage cross-talk. Some (such as Save the Last Word for Me and the Four A's) include specific structures for people to respond to each other and time for open conversation.[15] However, by definition, following a protocol is not free form. To some people, the structure can seem overly rigid and dictatorial, particularly protocols that include time limits. They serve an important purpose, however. McIntosh describes the serial testimony structure as "the autocratic administration of time in the service of democratic distribution of time."[16] Too often during discussions about race and racism, a few people—usually white, often male—take up more than their share of airtime. Others hold back because they don't want to appear rude by interrupting someone. The framework of a conversation structure serves to protect the valuable resource of time so that it is shared equally.

Protocols have made a difference at CCPCS, where the K–12 staff requires a large number of small-group facilitators. Knowing that protocols will guide their work, however, makes it easier for people to step up to facilitate. Sixteen staff members regularly volunteer to facilitate discussions with ten to twelve of their peers. With predetermined prompts, time limits, and a sequence to the conversation, facilitators need to make fewer decisions on their own. School leaders acknowledge that volunteer facilitators don't always know how to push the conversation deeper to ensure everyone is leaning into discomfort. Sometimes, following the protocol isn't enough. However, some conversation is better than none. Meanwhile, leaders continue to invest in the facilitators and their own development and expect that group members will increasingly build capacity to consistently push themselves and their groups.

Provide Practice Talking About Race Through Realistic Scenarios

The Equity Core Committee at Capital City maintains its stance that equity meetings are, in order of priority, focused on self, then on building the skills to have conversations about race and equity within the community, and last on developing specific teaching practices. In addition to using protocols to respond to a variety of texts, the Equity Committee designed two structures to allow teachers to practice applying new insights to real-world contexts.

The committee wrote scenarios based on common school situations. During the sessions, people break into pairs or trios, and teachers role-play how they might respond to each specific situation. For example, in one scenario, a child of color tells the teacher she's being racist because she sends him to the office more often than white students. In another scenario, a white parent requests that her child not be placed with a black teacher because she "just doesn't seem like the right fit for her daughter." In the role-play, teachers don't theorize what they *would* say; they actually say it out loud and practice talking about race in high-stakes situations involving students, parents, and colleagues.

Role-playing the situation requires teachers to practice using language appropriate to their grade level, trying out different responses, and hearing their peers' ideas for responses as well. Teachers doing role-plays might also brainstorm multiple possible responses and then choose one to act out. Reflecting on the role-plays together involves listening to different perspectives, considering different approaches, becoming more aware of how identity influences daily interactions, and widening personal lenses.

The CCPCS Equity Core Committee also invited teachers to bring dilemmas of practice to their groups. As trust has built among the group members, teachers increasingly bring dilemmas to their groups: *"Yesterday a child said this to me and I didn't know how to respond."* A teacher will present the dilemma that involves race in some way and then, using a consultancy protocol, hear her colleagues analyze and give feedback. Through role-plays and dilemmas, teachers practice what they may not have practiced anywhere else. As Dresden, the head of school, says, "Staff members build up skills for how to handle a situation before it happens. At the same time, they develop their ability to have courageous conversations with colleagues across differences."

TALKING ABOUT RACE THROUGHOUT THE DAY

Dresden explains why her staff has committed to ongoing discussions of race rather than periodic trainings:

> It shouldn't be that we're talking about writing and then later we talk about equity. It should be the lens that we look at everything through. It shouldn't be a separate thing. We need to give people the language and a tool kit to incorporate this into their mindset, to continually raise good questions. So that if we're looking at the reading data, this is the lens that people bring and that informs the questions that they ask. Through our ongoing equity work, we work on developing that lens that then hopefully becomes the way we're looking at things all the time.[17]

Shifting from a colormute and color-blind school culture to one where all school staff naturally consider race and bias throughout their work takes time. As with learning a new language, educators need structured practice before they become fluent. Using staff meetings and team meetings to hold scheduled, structured conversations about race ensures that everyone gets a minimum amount of practice to prepare them to talk about race beyond these meetings. When Tracey was a high school principal in a school where 100 percent of his leadership team and classroom teachers were white, he came to realize that his staff needed more support to make this culture shift.

While Tracey initially decided not to directly address race himself, he hired an outside organization to lead several conversations about race and racism with his faculty. He was concerned, however, that the conversations weren't permeating the work of the school. His faculty had very little experience talking about race. He noticed a pattern of some staff being absent on those staff meeting days. It was clearly going to take more strategic planning to help the staff become more comfortable talking about race.

Tracey engaged his leadership team, which included all department chairs, as a critical lever for change. They were, for the most part, reflective teachers willing to support this work. Tracey specifically asked them to name race when they led department meetings, when they were helping a teacher plan a lesson or find a resource, and throughout their work with the teachers they supervised.

Tracey didn't just leave it there, however. At each weekly leadership team meeting, Tracey reserved time for people to report about the conversations they were having: "I noticed that a group of black girls always sits in the back of American History class. I asked Mr. Johnston about it, and he said he hadn't noticed. We're going to meet next week to talk about how to engage them more in the lesson." "I asked everyone in my department to bring their grading records, and we looked at the racial makeup of the top and bottom quartiles to look for patterns. Then we brainstormed what to do to change the patterns." The weekly check-ins at leadership meetings kept the need to talk about race front and center in people's minds. It helped spread the conversation throughout the day, throughout the school.

As with any teaching endeavor, we need to know the learners—in this case, the educators at our school. What is their experience talking about race, together as a staff? What skills do they need to be able to have these conversations? In some schools, naming and discussing race may already be a normal part of everyday conversation. For most schools, however, leaders need to make a deliberate plan to normalize talking about race as a staff. Leaders need to help teachers develop the basic building blocks of learning to talk about race together and (primarily for white teachers) understand that we all have a racialized experience. To do this, concrete structures like protocols, role-plays, and modeling help.

Another factor in schools' ability to normalize race talk is teachers' ability to take risks with each other. As risky as it may feel for some teachers to talk about race with colleagues, it's going to require even more courage to collaboratively examine ways actions may be racially biased. To create the conditions for this to happen, leaders will need to lean into the discomfort and cultivate brave communities.

GET IT WRONG IN ORDER TO GET IT RIGHT

The first attempts at leading conversations about race with a group of adults unaccustomed to such dialogues will likely not go as planned. The first dozen or so conversations will probably take all types of unexpected twists and turns. In most cases, as faculty and staff learn how to have these conversations, leaders are learning how to facilitate them. We can confirm from our own experience that it's scary to step into this unknown. However, as leaders, we've learned to take each mistake or wrong turn as a learning experience and forge ahead in service of eventually getting it right more often than getting it wrong.

CHAPTER 4

Cultivate a Brave Community

One reason educators need to be able to name race is so that they are equipped to examine their practice for racial bias. Addressing collective and individual unconscious racial biases as a school community requires breaking out of the racist/nonracist binary and viewing each other as learners on a developmental journey. When we as educators fail to do this—when we're judging others or protecting and defending our innocence from racial bias—we shut down learning and thus our own and others' ability to improve. Meanwhile, black and brown students continue to experience the impact of unchecked unconscious biases. For schools to fulfill our aspirations for all students, we need to truly invest in each others' learning. As James Baldwin wrote, "If I love you, I have to make you conscious of the things you don't see."[1] Let's move beyond the typical "culture of nice" in schools to reach a "culture of brave."

Education reform expert Richard Elmore describes a culture of nice as a community where people may smile and nod as their colleagues speak, while they simultaneously harbor significant doubts that they do not state publicly. This is one of the biggest stumbling blocks for any school improvement effort. No one wants to rock the boat. No one wants to be the one to bring up the uncomfortable truth that sits at every meeting. Instead, people prioritize maintaining harmony over sharing any comment or question that might cause disequilibrium.

As most of us know, the opposite of a culture of nice is not a "culture of mean." The opposite of the culture of nice is a community where people are willing to be honest with each other, to talk about hard topics, and to confront challenges together even when they're uncomfortable. Underlying honest interactions and challenging feedback is a belief in each others' capacity to learn. With a developmental view of our ability to tackle racism, we recognize that complacency is the enemy of improvement. A community that can tackle challenges head-on can learn to be more effective.

In an informative TED talk, commentator Jay Smooth likens pointing out bias to telling someone he has spinach in his teeth.[2] Wouldn't we all be relieved if our friends and colleagues told us about that leafy leftover that we didn't know was there? Sure, it's a little awkward, but we all understand the situation. We didn't put it there on purpose, we'd be happier if it weren't there, and we're glad to be able to address it. Smooth makes the case that we should be equally open to talking about our racial biases with each other and equally receptive to feedback about it. When Sarah's colleague pointed out that she was only noticing black students' side conversations, he didn't make her feel like a bad person; he was trying to help her. As a result, he improved her practice and the experience of students of color in her class. Unfortunately, for most of us, this kind of interaction is rare.

Consider the following examples from Sarah's school:

- During a meeting to discuss a black child who is not making progress, a teacher says, "Well, there's probably a TV in every room in the house and so it's going to be hard for him to concentrate." This teacher's colleague, who was in the meeting, came to Sarah's office later to share what she'd heard and her concern that her colleague was making assumptions based on no actual information. The teacher said she hadn't felt comfortable saying anything at the meeting and wouldn't have known what to say anyway.
- A special educator privately expressed concern to Sarah that a classroom teacher was overly quick to refer black students for special education. She'd noticed a pattern over the years, but had never said anything. She felt that saying something would only make the teacher feel attacked and would harm their ability to work with each other.
- Some black teachers were concerned about an excerpt from Lisa Delpit's *Other People's Children*, which Sarah shared with the staff.[3] They feared that it might have reinforced rather than dispelled stereotypes about black

students. They weren't sure of Sarah's motivations and goals and so at first hesitated to bring it up with her.

Scenarios like these are common occurrences in schools. Colleagues hold back from sharing a concern or asking a question for fear of triggering feelings of shame or defensiveness. In each case, the school's effectiveness is held back as well. What does it take to create a community where people feel able to raise concerns about bias in a way that doesn't feel like a personal attack? How do we cultivate a school culture where people regularly collaborate to investigate potential bias—their own and their school's—without fear of judgment? Is a culture like this even possible in schools?

We believe schools should embrace the ideals of what our colleague Janine de Novais calls a "brave" community where members of the community agree to push each other from a place of mutual respect and caring.[4] In successful brave communities, participants talk about their biases openly and ask risky questions without fear of being labeled ignorant, complicit, or racist. They challenge one another's perspectives without fear of being labeled aggressive or hurtful. This kind of honest, humble, curious, nondefensive learning culture doesn't happen on its own. Leaders deliberately cultivate it.

WHAT DOES A BRAVE COMMUNITY LOOK LIKE?

Few school leaders raised in American society have worked in a community that tackles unconscious racial bias head-on. It's just not something many of us have experienced—in any sector. It's hard to build something without knowing what it's supposed to look like when we're done. A teacher colleague of Tracey's shared a simple but instructive example of a time when she perceived bias at her school and spoke up about it. Her example provides a vision of what is possible.

One afternoon in Ms. Wilson's lively and joyful first-grade classroom, as children were assigned to new reading groups, a white girl announced loudly, "I don't want to be in a reading group with David because he's black." Ms. Wilson, who prided herself on actively affirming all racial backgrounds, was shocked. While comments like these happen periodically at many schools, she never expected it in her own classroom. She responded as best she could in the moment and later, after school, sat down at her computer to write some difficult emails. It pained her to have to tell the parents, but in a detailed email to David's and the white girl's parents, she explained what had happened.

In reply to the email, David's father asked to meet after school the next day. He arrived at the meeting with a notebook, pen, and a long list of questions. Still distressed that this had happened to his young child, he was unable to return Ms. Wilson's smile or warm greeting. He explained that he wanted to understand more about how the comment happened, what Ms. Wilson was doing about it, how she was teaching about racial identity in her classroom, and how she would work with the white girl, his son, and all the students going forward. As Ms. Wilson spoke, the father took notes.

Ms. Wilson, who is white, responded politely and as best as she could, but she found herself tongue-tied and intensely nervous during the meeting. When the father left, she immediately went to talk with the school counselor. She described the meeting and said she felt under attack. The father was hostile and clearly trying to intimidate her by taking notes on everything she said. The counselor, who is also a white woman, agreed that from Ms. Wilson's description, the father seemed aggressive and intimidating. She offered to join Ms. Wilson at any future meetings so she could feel safer.

Soon afterward, Ms. Wilson also explained the situation to Mrs. Richards, the school librarian and a close colleague, who is black. After listening to her colleague, Mrs. Richards reflected for a moment and then said, "You're my colleague, and I respect you, but I'm honestly worried that you view this man as aggressive. He has every right to ask for this information. He's devastated. He's hurting for his son and the fact that he can't protect him from such ugly comments. Of course, he wants to know more about what you're going to do. If this parent were white, would you feel afraid? White parents ask for this kind of meeting all the time and it's not a problem for us at this school. I wonder if you might be uncomfortable because he's asking about race and because he's a black man."

Mrs. Richards said it wasn't easy having this conversation with her colleague, but it also wasn't the first time she and her colleague had talked about race. She also felt she had to raise her concern for personal reasons. As someone with a black husband and nephew, she felt deeply and personally connected to the story. Our society's entrenched stereotypes about black men being aggressive were a direct threat to her family. She shared this with her colleague, and Ms. Wilson listened.

According to Mrs. Richards, hearing her colleague's account of this parent meeting was both discouraging and painful. However, she felt Ms. Wilson was genuinely open to hearing feedback. Her colleague was willing to acknowledge that she might have jumped to conclusions and that the father's behavior may have been less aggressive than she had perceived it to be. Ms. Wilson also confessed that despite staff conversations, talking about race is still scary for her and that she doesn't talk about race enough to feel confident talking about it with a black parent.

The conversation between these two colleagues opened up a lot, and they agreed to continue talking. Ms. Wilson said their conversation helped her see the way unconscious racial bias might have tainted her view of the meeting. She was still nervous, but she told the school counselor she didn't need her at future meetings with this parent, and she emailed to ask the father if he had any other questions. Over the course of the school year, the teachers continued to talk about this incident and Ms. Wilson's continuing and evolving reflections on it.

In some ways, this example is not unusual at all. What happened between the children is unfortunately common in US schools. The way the teacher interpreted the father's response is also not unusual. After all, one of our society's most common racist tropes is that of an aggressive or angry black man (particularly in relation to white women). We know that talking about race raises white people's anxieties and that these anxieties are heightened when a white person is having the discussion with a person of color.

However, in one significant way, this story is extremely uncommon: the teachers' ability to have this conversation about race and bias with each other. Mrs. Richards was able to speak about her concern directly, and her colleague was willing to hear and consider her perspective. This interchange should not be remarkable, but in our society, where race is so loaded, most of us would probably agree that it is. Mrs. Richards attributed their ability to have the conversation to the considerable trust they had established with each other. This was not the first time they shared honest feedback with each other, and it was not the first time they had talked about race together. They knew each others' family histories. They had shared their racial autobiographies. The trust they had established allowed them to be open and honest with each other, and this fostered better outcomes for their students.

Build Trust Through Challenging Interactions, Not Easy Ones

When addressing the charged topic of race, trust can be a deal breaker. It's also often misunderstood. Trust isn't built by hearing people's good intentions. Trust grows from witnessing people's actions. When we find ourselves in an uncomfortable situation with colleagues, and we agree to stay in the struggle with respect and honesty, we come out in a different place. We trust more.

Many people are familiar with adventure team-building activities that organizations sometimes hold for a day. People push themselves and take risks. They fall backward into their colleagues' arms for "trust falls," or jump off tall platforms in a harness held by their peers, or climb sheer walls with the support of their teammates below. In these activities, trust is built not through doing something comfortable with each other. People come to trust their teammates precisely because they feel afraid, take a leap into that fear, and find that their teammates remain with them. Relationships like the one between Mrs. Richards and Ms. Wilson are built through such interactions. When we know that we can count on our colleagues to stay with us, to partner with us to help us be our most courageous selves, charged conversations deepen rather than destroy our trust.

What is the equivalent of a trust fall when we're talking about racial bias? Demonstrating a willingness to speak honestly even when you fear that colleagues will turn their backs on you. Not turning your back on someone when she speaks honestly. Wanting to hear her truth. Receiving hard feedback about bias and not dismissing it. Being willing to tell someone when you see evidence of possible bias in his practice. Holding ourselves in a space that's uncomfortable for longer than we normally would.

Look online for advice for educators about addressing racism, and you'll almost always find an emphasis on safety. We agree that conversations need to be free of name-calling or personal slurs or threats, much the way we ensure that everyone is buckled into a harness while tackling the ropes course. However, safety in our collaborative work to address racism is often overemphasized and misunderstood. Too often, safety is conflated with feeling comfortable. When we're leaning back into trust falls or stepping off a platform on a zipline, we expect to feel that grip of anxiety, discomfort, self-doubt, heart-in-our-throat emotions. It's no different when we're supporting our staff to face the unconscious beliefs they don't know they have.

Educators especially know that easy and comfortable doesn't move us to the next level of understanding. Learning comes from grappling with a challenge, not eliminating it. If either Ms. Wilson or Mrs. Richards had taken the comfortable route, their interaction would not have led to the insights it did. Ms. Wilson wouldn't have accepted the uncomfortable feedback, and Mrs. Richards wouldn't have given it.

Use Norms to Encourage Bravery

Grappling with and not avoiding challenge takes conscious effort. One of our cohorts of aspiring principals generated the norm, "Value truth over comfort." Did they always follow it? No. However, the group that established this norm returned to it frequently and made great strides in speaking honestly about challenging topics including racism. They reminded each other to follow their shared norm and said when they felt they weren't adhering to their agreed-upon behavior.

People are bound to drop the ball at times. Working in groups is hard. As psychologists Robert Kegan and Lisa Lahey write, norms are valuable not because they magically lead to compliance. At least that's never been the case in any group we've been part of. The value of the norm is that by providing a clear boundary, we know when we've crossed it. As Kegan and Lahey write, norms make violations possible.[5] When norms can be violated, they can be reestablished. Without this violation, there's no means of recourse.

In his book, *Courageous Conversations About Race*, author Glenn Singleton recommends four "agreements of courageous conversation" that groups around the country have since used: stay engaged; experience discomfort; speak your truth; expect and accept nonclosure.[6] The agreements may seem innocuous. However, they can be very effective at catching us as we slip into common habits when talking about race in mixed-race groups.

Norms are a particularly useful tool in talking about our biases because most of us have bad habits in these conversations. Our binary racist/nonracist mindset kicks in, and we sort people, make judgments, check out, or respond in a host of other ways. When the right norms are in place, they make it possible for us to hold each other accountable for new and more courageous patterns of engagement.

Without norms like those set out by Singleton or our group of graduate students, people who don't speak their truth can claim that they were just being polite, that they didn't want to trouble the water, they didn't think people would want to hear. When the norms aren't in place, some group members are pushy, others are passive. However, when colleagues have explicitly named behaviors they do and don't want to see, they're empowered to hold each other and themselves accountable—to call people out when they fall back on old habits: "We haven't heard from you, David, and we agreed to stay engaged. Can you share what's going on for you now?" "I wasn't abiding by our norm last week when we were talking about the school-to-prison pipeline. I didn't say anything even though I had a strong reaction." "I need to ask a question that makes me uncomfortable, but I'm valuing truth over comfort." "I'm going to try to lean into discomfort today. It makes me nervous though."

Norms remain just words on chart paper, however, if we don't tend to them actively. As Singleton recommends, we ask people to check in on norms frequently in our work with groups. Which one was hardest for you? Which one did you violate today? Why? Did you see an example of someone following a norm in a way that helped the group? Over time, as we draw attention to the behaviors named in our norms, we expect people to become more self-aware and therefore more able to monitor their behaviors and build new skills.

At Capital City Public Charter School, teachers developed a norm to speak directly to each other when they see or hear evidence of potential racial bias. They call it the "forty-eight-hour rule." They developed the norm because they needed some structure to help people break out of the culture of nice and be able to approach a colleague with a concern. Teachers also agreed that feedback needed to happen soon for it to be helpful. The rule states that staff members commit to raising a concern within forty-eight hours of it happening, and colleagues agree to welcome the feedback. If you don't bring your concern directly to the person within forty-eight hours, you agree to let it go.

As Head of School Dresden explains,

Everyone knows that not *receiving* feedback is not good. But another thing that's really toxic for a school is that someone holds onto something. You wonder why someone is really cold to you, and you can't understand it. It's burdensome for both people and isn't good for culture. It's important for the person to say it, and it's important for the person to hear it. The forty-eight-hour rule is a way of signaling we're going to be a community where we talk about these things, it's one of our norms in our work. The term "courageous conversation" has helped. People say, "Can we have a courageous conversation?" It doesn't make it easy but it makes it seem more feasible.[7]

Build Trust by Engaging

As part of our work teaching aspiring principals, we attended a workshop about race and racism jointly with our students. Throughout the course of the workshop, participants were prompted to share their racialized experiences. People of color told personal stories of what it's like to be the only person of color in a group, to maintain composure after someone makes a statement that denies what you experience daily, and to experience self-doubt because of a lifetime of subtle and not so subtle messages describing your capacity as limited. Tracey shared his experience of looking in the mirror and realizing that the tall black man he sees is exactly the image that most white people fear—the boogeyman that haunts their nightmares.

After the workshop, we debriefed the experience with Cesar Cruz, one of the facilitators and a man of color. We talked about the courage of those who were willing to be so vulnerable and share stories that were clearly traumatizing. At one point, Cesar turned directly to Sarah and sincerely (and pointedly) asked, "How did you lean into discomfort at the workshop?" As soon as he asked the question, Sarah understood. That single, direct question turned out to be an enormous gift.

In considering her response, Sarah realized that she hadn't leaned into discomfort during the workshop. She'd chosen the safe role of observer. As one of the cohort's leaders, she told herself it was important to listen to others' stories. Besides, it seemed there wasn't much to tell beyond what was obvious: as a white person, she experienced enormous privilege. When Cesar asked that question, however, she realized that wasn't the whole story. Of course, there was more to share. What was her experience as a white person trying to understand and address racism in schools? In herself? What were her fears and doubts? What feelings came up for her in this work? In this conversation? In her own daily walk as a white person? She hadn't pushed herself to gain new insights about how race affected her daily experience. She hadn't leaned in to the opportunity to learn more about herself, even if it meant being uncomfortable with what she saw. She hadn't fully adhered to the norm of "speak your truth."

This imbalance in conversations about racial bias is common. We see the same pattern play out repeatedly. People of color take risks to share personal—sometimes painful—experiences or frank reflections, and white people passively listen. At the end of the conversation, white people can walk out of the room and never think about the conversation again. People of color live the conversation in their daily experience.

Silence carries different weight for people of color and for white people in conversations about race. White people often don't realize what a risk people of color take when they open up about their experiences. If the group they're in is typical of most groups of white Americans, personal sharing comes at a high cost. White listeners will likely question the perspective of people of color, doubt their experience, and/or deny aspects of their identity. Why would a person of color choose to enter a conversation with these risks?

What leads a person of color to take this risk? It's not a matter of trusting that the white colleague won't be biased. On the contrary, most people of color realistically expect some form of bias to show up in the conversation. Instead, what typically leads a person of color to open up in these conversations is believing that his or her efforts will somehow begin to chip away at the mountain of racism that confronts people of color every day. What can white people do to partner in this work? Engage.

We're not suggesting that white people engage by critiquing or doubting someone's personal experience. This is another common behavior of white people in conversations about race. In that case, silence would be a better option. However, often white silence comes from simply not leaning into discomfort. Even when a white person doesn't know what to say, that in and of itself is something to say: "To be honest, I feel anxious every time the topic of race comes up because I am worried that I'll say something wrong" or "This conversation makes me realize that I am not thinking about race very often and that my experience is not shared by everyone." Simply saying something to enter the conversation, instead of sitting silently listening to internal self-talk that adds to already heightened levels of anxiety, can build the self-assurance necessary to continue speaking and engaging. It also demonstrates at least a minimal willingness to take responsibility for learning so that people of color aren't left carrying that responsibility entirely on their own.

Taking up all the air space is not the goal either. Unfortunately, there isn't a playbook for knowing how much to talk. However, white people can pay attention to their motivations for participating or not. If fear is involved in keeping silent, it's worth examining rather than running away from it. If self-justification is involved, it's usually a good sign to stop talking and listen more.

WHEN WE'RE BRAVE, WE DON'T DENY BIAS

A white administrator going through unconscious bias training shared an interaction he regretted. During a meeting in the principal's office, a distraught mother accused this principal, saying, "You don't care about my daughter because she's black." Feeling as if he'd been punched in the stomach, the principal immediately refuted this parent's claim. The meeting ended acrimoniously.

Later, after learning about unconscious bias, this principal reflected that he wished he'd responded differently. He wished he'd acknowledged his potential bias and asked the parent more about what she saw that led her to that conclusion. He wished he'd told her that any biased actions she'd noticed were not aligned with his beliefs and were things he wanted to change.

White leaders may worry that acknowledging potential bias introduces a problem not already there. On the contrary, as Beverly Daniel Tatum describes, parents of color may be reassured when a white educator names race or bias, not because it means the person is free from bias, but because it indicates that the person may be aware of his or her own prejudices.[8] Clearly, this is only one factor in building a trusting relationship, but it can be helpful when a person in authority acknowledges a problem that so many families of color face.

White leaders spend too much time trying to prove they're not racist. Instead of reducing blind spots, this strategy only reinforces them. Rather than deny or suppress feedback, leaders need to see feedback much the way growth mindset guru Carol Dweck would encourage a learner to see feedback: as an opportunity to learn and grow.[9]

Thus, when a person of color questions a white leader on his or her thinking, the leader has an opportunity to practice and model nondefensiveness.

Robin DiAngelo, a scholar on race and racism who is a white woman, describes two ways she responds when she gets feedback about her biases from a person of color:

1. How, where, and when you give me feedback is irrelevant—it is the feedback I want and need. Understanding that it is hard to give, I will take it any way I can get it. From my position of social, cultural and institutional white power and privilege, I am perfectly safe and I can handle it. If I cannot handle it, *it's on me* to build my racial stamina.
2. Thank you.[10]

Another simple way to counteract the impulse to be defensive is to ask for more information. Can you tell me more about what makes you say that? What else do I need to know? Recognizing that we're learners requires recognizing that we make mistakes. A developmental mindset leads to seeing mistakes as moments when we're on the cusp of significant learning. Helping ourselves and our staff adopt this perspective strengthens our ability to collaborate productively and bravely.

Model Bravery by Owning Bias

School leaders have many opportunities to model a nondefensive learner's approach to acknowledging and monitoring their biases. For instance, when the school counselor and Sarah were filing reports with the state for child neglect, Sarah would question whether they were proceeding more quickly with a family of color than with a white family. When she and her secretary chatted about the day's visitors to the office, they asked themselves whether they were judging a low-income family of color as pushy, whereas the same action by a more affluent, white family appeared to be advocacy. When allocating school resources, Sarah invited others to join in the thought experiment of asking what kinds of decisions the school would make if the students in greatest need were affluent white students.

Naming our bias in a one-on-one situation is one thing. Standing in front of a large group and naming that we have unconscious racial bias can feel like an impossibly hard leadership challenge, particularly for white leaders who want so badly to be recognized as good white people.

Sarah learned from an experience she had teaching aspiring principals. She was explaining that leaders can't simply let racial disparities continue. They need to take action, and if that means taking more on their plate, so be it. She gave an example of a policy she instituted regarding parent conferences. Her school had a disproportionate number of families of color not participating. To remedy this, Sarah told teachers that if the parents didn't sign up, even after repeated calls, teachers should pass the contact information on to the office. Sarah would call personally to ensure that all parents knew about the school's expectations for 100 percent participation in family conferences and to ask what the school could do to make this happen. If parents were working two jobs or didn't have a car or otherwise couldn't come, Sarah could help reschedule the time and place for the conference.

After giving this example, Sarah could tell that something had hit a nerve because there was a low murmur of several people reacting disapprovingly to the comment. Sarah's heart sank. The example was supposed to demonstrate how to decrease inequities and (to be really honest) to signal her position as a good white person working to disrupt racial disparities in school. Instead, it seemed to have had the opposite effect. As she sensed the reaction in the room, she felt a combination of frustration that people wouldn't trust her good intentions (there it is again!) and concern that people would lose trust in her ability to address racial inequities.

In that moment, Sarah could hear Cesar asking, "How have you leaned into discomfort?" Even though it was just a few minutes before the end of class, Sarah told herself that this was one of those moments. She had to own her blind spots and open herself up to learning. Hearing from people directly would be better than knowing they were talking about it in the halls and parking lot. It was also clear that this could be a learning experience for her students as well. What made it particularly challenging, however, was that Sarah's learning had to be so public.

With a leap into the unknown, she said to the group, "I sense that some people were uncomfortable with what I just said. What did I miss? Please help me understand what I'm not seeing." Immediately, three hands shot into the air, all from people of color. These educators explained that they felt the example had assumed the parents of color were all low-income, thus reinforcing a stereotype that had followed them their whole lives. Could it be instead that the school was doing something that made families of color less inclined to come to conferences?

In that moment, Sarah was tempted to explain, defend, or otherwise justify her comments. Instead, with effort, she listened and thanked people for the honest feedback. (The fact that class was ending helped Sarah bite her tongue as well.)

In quieter moments after class, Sarah could see that her comments (and likely underlying beliefs) conflated people of color and low-income families and surfaced a careless and potentially harmful association. As the leader of the group, she wondered what would come next. Would people continue to trust her leadership? Were people somewhat distant as they walked out the door? Did fewer people say goodbye as they left or was it just perception?

The result of this interaction was that people of color and white people in the group were more—not less—willing to talk to Sarah about race, to share their experiences, and to raise something she might have missed. If she had explained away or denied the feedback, she would have lost an opportunity to learn about her blind spots and the experiences of people of color from this and subsequent interactions.

In a conversation about race, when a person of color is willing to raise a concern, to stay in the conversation and share a personal perspective, this is a valuable opportunity for learning. Sarah's defensive impulses haven't disappeared. However, with the growing understanding of what a liability these impulses are, it becomes easier to manage them.

In this situation, the listeners would have had every right to feel angry that a leader had just reinforced an association that people of color regularly have to battle. Refraining from defensiveness would have been more difficult if people had been angry. Hopefully, however, this anger wouldn't have changed Sarah's response: "I appreciate your feedback. I appreciate your willingness to share it. It's helping me see my blind spots, which I need to become more aware of." It wouldn't have been easy, but the learning would have remained the same.

Tracey has also come to see the value of leaders being open about their biases. Looking back on his time as a principal, Tracey wishes he had said some variation of "I don't know how to have these conversations together about the racial disparities at our school, but I know they're important. Let's learn together." He wished he'd felt more comfortable telling staff about his own racial uncertainties: "I'm working on my own biases about white people as stuck in beliefs and unable to change. I know this is something I need to work on and I'm committed to doing it."

Finally, he would have asked the outside consultant to work with him as well as with the staff. He would have acknowledged that he needed help, and doing so might have taught him to engage teachers in leading the work with him. Instead, as the only champion of addressing racial inequalities, when Tracey left, the work at his school ended. Interestingly, at the end of his tenure, his staff completed a 360-degree survey of his leadership, and he learned that people had wanted him to share more of his own struggles so they could relate to him more. People respected him and wanted to learn more about his thinking.

Now, Tracey regularly tells groups about his experience facing his own bias with black students in the high school hallways at passing time. Hearing a leader of color explain that he has biases, too, has a profound effect on a group. Hearing how he accepted student feedback, investigated further, and acknowledged his biases provides a clear example for educators to follow.

Brave communities don't just happen. Leaders deliberately build them. They model bravery and prioritize trust building. They recognize that leaning into discomfort strengthens rather than threatens a community. Throughout it all, they clearly communicate the developmental nature of the work. Courageous conversations aren't about proving that we as educators are right. Rather they establish us as committed to continual improvement. In this way, they can be seen as freeing. We're all influenced by bias. Let's have the courage to face this and help reduce the effects of this bias on students. Let's not hide our blind spots but help each other see and address them. Let's be brave together.

CHAPTER 5

Whose Comfort Are We Prioritizing?

So far, we've described a bold vision for leadership. School leaders foster a brave community where teachers talk about race and the ways racial bias lives in all of us. This work is challenging and will undoubtedly raise a range of feelings among staff members. Leaders need to be prepared for a strong reaction. When unanticipated, strong feelings from staff members can throw a leader off course or cause a leader to abandon ship. In this chapter, we seek to prepare leaders for the various forms of resistance that may surface—both overt and subtle—in response to this work.

WHITE FRAGILITY: THE DESIRE TO MAINTAIN A SENSE OF COMFORT

We recently led a workshop on how school leaders can address unconscious racial bias in their schools. When we asked participants to identify the primary barriers they face in this work, a black man immediately replied, "The need to keep white people comfortable." People of color around the room nodded their heads in emphatic agreement.

Scholar Robin DiAngelo coined the phrase "white fragility" to describe white people's desire to maintain a sense of comfort and ease while addressing racism.[1] She describes the corresponding forms of resistance that get triggered when white people begin to feel uncomfortable or disoriented, which predictably happens when people learn that their perception of the world is not always trustworthy. This concept helps us understand why conversations about race and racism often end up lingering in spaces that are meant to ensure that white people are comfortable. For example, it's easier for mixed-race or all-white groups to talk about overt racism or historical racism, but white people often become defensive when addressing the ways racism operates today and the ways they've internalized it in the form of unconscious bias. White people tend to resist the idea that unconscious racial bias influences their decisions, actions, justifications, and rationale and may cause harm.

We also helped facilitate a conversation about racial identity with a group of teachers, and at one point the conversation got emotionally charged. A white teacher said she didn't want to talk about racism or what her experience was as a white person. With exasperation, she explained that she was already sacrificing a lot of comforts to teach poor children of color. She could have an easier teaching job in the suburbs, but she had chosen to teach in the inner city. Wasn't that enough to prove she wasn't racist? A black colleague responded firmly, "If that's how you feel, then I don't want you teaching my children. You should teach in the suburbs instead." The white teacher started to cry as the conversation moved on.

At the end of this session, a number of people went to comfort the white teacher. Later, the black teacher told Sarah what it had felt like to watch people's response: "I feel like a pariah. Everyone is checking in with her, and no one is talking to me. I feel like people think I did something wrong. Like people think I attacked her. I thought our norm was 'speak your truth' and that's what I was trying to do. But now it feels like people are shunning me."

This was a sign that the group needed to learn about white fragility and the potential to either reinforce it or help move peers through and past it. In that moment, the white woman didn't need reassurance that she was a good person. Instead, she needed peers to support her in staying in that discomfort.

As this example points out, it's not just the facilitator who enforces a desire for comfort; participants influence where and how the conversation goes as well. Even the way people interact with each other after a discussion—or in the in-between moments—can reinforce the status quo. As leaders, we need to be alert to the common pattern of trying to reduce or eliminate white discomfort, which only reinforces inequities. Brave communities require that we normalize the discomfort in these conversations, not reduce it.

Our colleagues at Capital City Public Charter School caution about this topic in the facilitator notes for their equity orientation for new staff: "This work is hard. Expect to experience discomfort—it is part of the process. Our role as facilitators is to push thinking while ensuring the safety of the group— not to make everyone feel comfortable."

If we as leaders are going to grow, we're going to have to experience a fair amount of disequilibrium with our current thinking. Like crabs, we're going to need to grow uncomfortable in our own shell before naturally shedding it to move to the next stage of development.

Capital City Head of School Dresden explains that letting people stay in this discomfort is one of the challenges for her as a white leader:

> Part of this work is discomfort especially for white colleagues who may be new to this work. Letting people feel discomfort is a good thing and can lead to growth. It's not my job to make you feel better. That's been one of the biggest learnings from this work. We had an example where a black staff member shared a concern with her white colleague. She thought this colleague had treated some black students unfairly during lunch time and told her. It affected the colleague so deeply. It was very painful. I had to remember it's not my job to make her feel better. She was beating herself up about it and my instinct was to say, "You're not a bad person, you had good intentions." But I remember that for me a lot of my growth has come from times when I have just felt awful. Part of the process is realizing that sometimes you're just not going to feel good and reflecting on discomfort is how you grow. As the school leader, I have to remember that it's not my job to make you feel better. If you want to talk about it, we can talk about it, but I'm not going to try to make you feel better.[2]

Dresden ended up telling this white staff member that she'd been given a gift. Her black colleague could have shunned her, talked about her to black colleagues, and never shared personal observations or feelings. Dresden told the white colleague, "You have to understand that when your colleague tells you something like this, she's giving you a gift by telling you what she experienced. You can own it, you can really listen." Unfortunately, this white colleague withdrew from the black colleague after this incident. Dresden expects things to improve, but acknowledges that everyone has to do his or her own work.

The discomfort that comes when white people face the ways they've internalized racism can be intense. In chapter 2, we described how Sarah experienced white fragility in her interactions with Tracey. It was hard to face the possibility that despite her love for her students, she may have traumatized them. The white woman in the workshop described earlier and the white teacher at Capital City probably felt something similar. It's disorienting and devastating, so it's not surprising that a first response is to push back or withdraw: "But that can't be! I care about my students. You are painting a picture of me that is ugly, frightening, and utterly foreign to me and something I am loathe to accept."

Despite how painful this feels to white people, there's clearly no comparison to the experience of people of color who live in a society that continually marginalizes or denies their experience. Sarah finds that she can manage her discomfort better when she remembers what Tracey said to her one afternoon when they were discussing how to facilitate a conversation about racism: "I have to feel uncomfortable every day. I'm uncomfortable when I'm at a meeting and my comments are ignored until a white colleague repeats them, when my colleague talks about 'those families' and he's talking about people who look like me, when I enter the elevator and a white woman holds her purse tightly, when I go to a restaurant and the wait staff address themselves to my white colleague and not me. I don't think it's too much to ask for white people to feel uncomfortable for an hour or two." On that day, listening to Tracey's long list, Sarah realized the unfairness of trying to maintain comfort in conversations about race. She made a silent pledge to step up and be willing to be uncomfortable more often. Even with this pledge, the pull to remain comfortable is constant.

Avoid Keeping Conversations Superficial for the Facilitator's Comfort

As leaders, how do we help staff members—particularly those who are white—lean in to this uncomfortable place rather than avoid it? Too often, as leaders, we enable white people's comfort by keeping conversations about racism at a superficial level. For example, several years ago, Sarah showed her graduate class the now well-known video of a white police officer in South Carolina forcibly removing a silent black student from her seat in class before arresting her. As the graduate students discussed the video, most people clearly felt that the police officer showed a shockingly inappropriate use of force against a student. However, Sarah sensed that a few students in class disagreed, although they never raised their hands. Rather than invite what most likely would have been different perspectives into the room, Sarah brought the conversation to a close and moved on.

No one in Sarah's class could claim that voices were explicitly silenced during the discussion. However, no one could make the case that racism was effectively challenged either. Sarah realized later that of course everyone knew those differing perspectives were in the room. By not inviting them into the conversation, she was complicit in allowing them to continue. At a minimum, she didn't help these aspiring principals analyze the situation and their conclusions critically.

If we as leaders are going to shift thinking, we need to create opportunities for people to be brave. When Tracey attends workshops where the white facilitator talks about racism superficially, he takes the initiative to ask a question or share a personal experience that prompts deeper discussion. Often it falls to people of color to do this. However, this shouldn't be the job of Tracey or other people of color attending the workshop. As facilitators of any race, we need to design learning experiences that ensure direct discussion, analysis, and reflection regarding race and racism. When planning discussions, Sarah's initial impulse is still to protect her own and other white people's comfort. This impulse persists. However, the concept of white fragility helps her recognize this tendency now and pushes her to dig deeper, to seek out the questions or tasks that require people to question their own perspective: "What if you were the principal in this situation, another student in the classroom, the parent of this student? What exactly might you think and what would you say?" Effective questions push people to surface and examine their discomfort: "Why might you avoid taking this action step? Who loses when you do or do not take this step? Who gains?"

Sarah is learning to ask herself, "Whose comfort am I privileging?" When we as leaders enable superficial conversations about racism, we're privileging white people's comfort. We're ignoring the discomfort people of color in the room may experience from the silence about racism and the discomfort students of color are likely experiencing from our unexamined biases. As leaders and facilitators of any race, when we avoid heated conversations, we're privileging our own desire for comfort over the daily experiences of staff and students of color.

Centering white comfort and keeping conversations superficial is not unique to white people. Leaders of color may do the same thing. However, for people of color, this is often a matter of survival—in organizations, in friendships, and in daily life. Like most people of color, Tracey continually monitors the level of discomfort of white people in his interactions. It's especially pertinent for a black man who likely triggers a range of unconscious biases in white people (especially white women). Tracey weighs the pros and cons of speaking his truth depending on the purpose and context: "Will the person shut down if I continue to probe? Can this person stay in their discomfort a bit longer or are they about to disengage? Do I want to share my experience of being dismissed in meetings? Am I prepared to experience another white person denying my reality?" Questions like these come up not just in one-on-one conversations but also as self-preservation questions at work where the impact could have long-term professional repercussions. He must ask himself, "Do I want to operate right now as an agitator or a teacher or do I just want to go about my work without the 'racial battle fatigue' that too often comes from conversations with white people about race?"

When people of color raise hard questions, point out potential bias, and lean into discomfort, they're doing that on top of the daily marginalization they experience. These interactions do not happen on a level playing field. What we as leaders ask of our staff of color has a different impact than what we ask of white staff members. The consequences of not having these conversations are different for these two groups as well.

Avoid Centering White People's Comfort

One of the most persistent theories we hear—and that we ourselves have succumbed to at different times—is that addressing racism or bias directly with our faculty will do more harm than good. At the very least, leaders fear it will cause a mess and uncertainty about how to clean it up. People might become offended, personal connections will fray, people will take sides and start divisions, and wounds will be created, reopened, and left to fester. We've also heard white colleagues defend this position by saying, "It's not that I'm trying to protect my white teachers. They probably need to hear some hard truths. It's that I just don't want to subject my teachers of color to another traumatizing conversation."

What's missing from this rationale is that a community's silence about race is demeaning and dehumanizing, too. The notion that we can avoid discomfort is a largely white perspective that ignores the effects of racism that people of color experience every day. After all, people of color endure plenty of ignorant or offensive comments (most probably unintentional) from white people; that's nothing new. As shown in chapter 1, they also have to navigate a society that regularly treats people of color differently from white people. Rather than protection, most educators of color seek conversations that surface rather than sidestep prejudice. They're less afraid of the churn that can happen during a difficult conversation about race and racism. At least it's being addressed.

One of the simplest and most effective ways that white fragility inhibits progress is through passive avoidance, persistently postponing the work: "We'll tackle this next month. Next year. When things settle. When we don't have a new curriculum. When we have more bandwidth. Fewer district meetings. Additional staff development days."

A colleague of ours told about her principal's attempts to hold a full-staff meeting on unconscious racial bias. It was originally scheduled for the summer retreat. As the retreat approached, the principal ran out of time to prepare for the session, so moved it to the first month of school. Something else came up that seemed more urgent, so he put it off until October. When it was postponed to November, our colleague knew that it was more than just calendaring that was getting in the way. She raised her concern with the principal and suggested that even if the reasons were legitimate, repeatedly postponing the meeting was sending a clear message to staff that this topic was not a priority. The principal got the message, and the session happened in November, which at least opened the door for conversations.

A white principal and colleague of Sarah's asked for advice when he felt tension at his school between the mostly black assistant teachers and the mostly white staff. He knew emotions were brewing under the surface. White administrators talked about it as an issue of the assistants feeling like second-class citizens because they were not lead teachers, but it was clear that race was a part of the tension as well. Yet this principal had avoided using staff time to address the tension or talk about race: "It will be too messy, it will bring up hard feelings, it will divide us."

After hearing about the situation, Sarah suggested that it sounded as if the black members of his staff already had hard feelings and already felt a sense of division. So whose comfort was he really protecting? After a long pause, this principal let out a slow breath and said, "Thank you." He hadn't recognized his unconscious prioritizing of the white perspective and thanked Sarah for pointing out this blind spot. He wasn't ready to facilitate the work himself but arranged for an outside organization to do work on racial equity with the full staff.

School leaders will always have too much to schedule. Leaders constantly face decisions about what to prioritize, what deserves the precious resource of faculty time. This work has to be a priority or it will never rise to the top of the list.

Capital City middle school principal Laina Cox explains why she proactively reserves time for staff to talk about race and racism, even as she struggles to fit everything into her professional development calendar:

> I have prioritized this work because everything else falls under it. We're talking about training the people [teachers] who are leading everything else in the school. If they have unaddressed bias, then they're impacting student discipline, learning, test performance, etc. It's all being impacted by the teacher standing in front of the kids. If we don't do the unconscious bias work, it's undermining all of our other work. So it's about naming our priorities. If you are not having these types of conversations, the issues that are going to arise will take more time. You're going to constantly be putting out fires because you're going to be using more time addressing these issues.[3]

Cox says her school gets creative about how it allocates time. As one small example, the administrators realized that equity teams required time to build the trust needed to have deep, personal conversations. So, on a curriculum planning day, Capital City provides lunch for the staff and asks them to sit with their equity teams. "We find pockets of time and use them," Cox says.

Provide Compassion, Not Coddling

Most educators are helpers; we want to help when we see someone struggle. This can be a liability when we're trying to lean into rather than avoid discomfort. People—likely most white staff—will struggle as they learn about their own unconscious racial biases and the ways they may harm students. As leaders, we need to resist the temptation to make it easier. As educators know best, struggle is often the place of learning. Struggle often leads to powerful insight. When people grapple with internal conflict—"But this isn't what I thought . . . This doesn't line up with my worldview"—they often come out on the other end with new perspectives. As educators, that's the outcome we're looking for.

In brave communities, people of color will often be on the receiving end of a white person's struggle with white fragility. In these situations, how does a person of color respond to a white colleague with compassion but not coddling? For example, consider the two situations we witnessed in our work:

- During a structured discussion about race, a white woman explained that she is learning that she may be causing harm because she is unaware of her unconscious racial biases. Her voice cracks and wavers as she shares that this is one of the most painful things she's learned about herself and she is grappling with all the implications. Her listening partner, who is black, shows great concern as she witnesses her partner's pain. She responds reassuringly, "I'm sure you're not causing harm. You seem like a very caring person. You're not causing harm."
- During a different structured conversation about race, two white women were visibly anxious and expressed their discomfort and embarrassment at not knowing how to talk about racism with adults or children. A black woman in their group said, "I want to appreciate you for sharing what you're sharing. I can tell it's uncomfortable and you could have stayed silent and you didn't. I hope you'll keep sharing."

Both situations involved people struggling and in discomfort. Many educators find it hard to leave that unattended. However, reassurance that everything is fine is not helpful. The first teacher needs to face the possible impact of her unconscious racial bias. Her students need her to face that uncomfortable truth so that she will feel compelled to reduce the negative impacts of those biases. In the second situation, the response honored the struggle without trying to eliminate it. It's that struggle that will lead to learning.

As white people strive to recognize the ways racism has subtly grown roots in their unconscious, people of color have no obligation to appreciate, encourage, or otherwise respond. People of color should not be expected to be the teacher, encourager, sympathizer, or cheerleader for white people facing their internalized racism. In formal or informal ways, people of color should never be expected to play that role.

The paradox, however, is that when people of color choose to step into the role of teacher, it can often lead to transformation for white people. Ask most white people how they came to a new understanding of their unconscious racial bias, and most will point to a person of color who was willing to—formally or informally—act as their teacher. What's often not recognized, however, is that this role of teaching comes at a cost. White people often don't understand or appreciate how emotionally taxing it is to repeatedly explain racism, white privilege, and white fragility. For people of color, the laborious process of explaining daily reality, of refuting doubts, of patiently helping a colleague unpack racist assumptions, all while encountering defensiveness and sometimes anger, leaves fewer personal resources for addressing the personal and professional challenges of any given day. No matter how well intentioned, when white people expect people of color to teach them about their biases, they reinforce existing inequities and unfairly burden their colleagues of color while benefiting themselves.

In addition to expecting people of color to do the teaching, another common pattern is that white people often don't do their homework. Tracey can describe countless times when he recommended that a white colleague or friend read an article, and the white person neglected to follow through. This leaves the burden for teaching solidly on the shoulders of the person of color. Over and over, Tracey has experienced interactions where white people continue to expect him to teach them and don't read what he's recommended, process it, and let him know what they learned from it. In addition, as Sarah learned in her experience described in chapter 2, reading what Tracey recommended at an academic level wasn't enough. She needed to think hard about the ways the concepts in the article applied to her own daily beliefs and actions. If white people want to reduce the burden on people of color to be their teachers, they've got to do some outside work.

The bottom line is that whether or not an educator of color takes on the role of teacher must be a choice. African American poet-performer Amanda Kemp explains an important distinction that guides her work in addressing racial inequities in education.[4] When she teaches white people about racism, she's very clear that she does it because it serves her mission, which is to increase love and justice in the world. In her workshops, she explains that this choice is crucial for her so that she feels empowered, not disrespected. We need to respect that teachers of color have a right to this decision as well. If they don't want to serve as teacher, they shouldn't be expected to.

Accept and Expect Nonclosure

Finally, we return to the final norm from Glenn Singleton's *Courageous Conversations*: accept and expect nonclosure.[5] One of the ways leaders support their staff is in helping them face the facts. We *all* harbor biases. We're all part of the problem. Again, we come back to commentator Jay Smooth's metaphor: getting rid of our unconscious racial bias is not like getting rid of tonsils: "It's no longer a problem—I removed it last year!" The work of addressing racial bias is like brushing our teeth every day.[6] Skillful leaders create brave communities where educators are prepared and supported to engage in this daily routine.

CHAPTER 6

Investigating the Racial Climate in Our Schools

Brave communities start from the premise that racial bias lives in our schools and ourselves every day. With that knowledge, the logical response is to be on the lookout for it. We all have to locate the ways it's impacting *our* students at *our* school and replace it with systems or structures that ensure fairness.

Ultimately, the goal is that every staff member incorporates alertness to racial equity into their work every day—the way they examine student achievement data, the questions they ask themselves at the end of a day of teaching, the way they look at students' work, the way they reflect on their day. Individual teachers might ask themselves: "Why don't I see black boys volunteering to solve a problem at the board? Are kids of color partnering up in my class because they want to or because they're shunned from other groups? Which students did I talk to today and who didn't I talk to and do I notice racial patterns?" At a team meeting, while reviewing quarterly assessment data, teachers might ask, "Why isn't the new intervention system helping our Latino/a girls catch up to grade level? Why didn't our new writing workshop approach work as well for our native students as it did for our other students?" A school's instructional leadership team might ask the following questions while reviewing longitudinal data: "Why do reading scores drop so significantly from second to third grade for many of our black students? On our school climate survey, why do our Latino boys repeatedly report that they do not have a single trusted adult at school?" The goal is for continuous inquiry into racial equity to become intuitive and integrated into the work we already do, not to be another initiative.

At the same time, it's helpful to designate at least some time and focus to specifically investigate racial bias. This ensures that a school builds the habit and investigates questions that may not come up without this specific attention. As with many continuous improvement efforts gaining momentum in education, the goal is to shift the focus from intentions to impact. The questions are not, "Do we care about our students of color? Do we have high aspirations and expectations for them?" Rather, the questions become, "How do students describe what they are experiencing in our classrooms and schools? What is the impact of our teaching on students? How do we know?"

Improving even just a few aspects of how students of color experience school could make a significant difference. As teachers make shifts in their practice that lead to improvements in students' learning and sense of belonging, they build a sense of agency that then leads to greater investment in ongoing racial equity inquiry.

Anyone familiar with action research or continuous improvement cycles will be familiar with the basic process. The inquiry starts with questions we want to learn more about based on a racial disparity we see in our school: "Does every student of color have a meaningful relationship with at least one adult? Why do fewer black and brown students visit the counselor's office in their junior year, and how can we ensure equal access to quality college counseling? Why are there more office referrals of black students from fifth-grade math class than fifth-grade science class and how do we reduce them?"

Then we investigate this racial disparity. We collect and analyze evidence, determine a root cause, design a system to reduce the impact of our biases on students in this particular area, check to see if it made a difference, and celebrate progress. If our improvement efforts don't produce results, we may not have identified the right area for focus or the right strategies to address it.

There is no formula for this inquiry process, other than the fact that it always starts and ends with data. When we want to discover something that is, by definition, unconscious, we can't rely on self-assessments of our own behavior. In our own experience, we've seen schools create action plans for teachers to "monitor their own biases." This is like asking someone who is medically diagnosed as colorblind to monitor for when they misidentify green as red. The point is that *they can't see it*. They'll always need to look at some other data source to know whether their color identification is accurate. The same thing applies to unconscious racial bias. We can't see it in ourselves. We need external data to help us identify whether our behaviors are truly fair.

Unlike other kinds of improvement cycles, investigating potential racial bias carries an emotional element as well. Learning that we may be part of the problem of low achievement for our students of color can feel disturbing and emotionally draining. Recognizing the ways we have absorbed society's racism and the ways this shows up in our daily actions requires self-awareness and stamina. We need to support our staff to engage productively in this work over the long term.

Framing makes a difference. As leaders, we need to be clear that our inquiry is not a gotcha exercise; the point is not to determine who is to blame. Instead, this process of collecting and analyzing data should feel empowering to teachers. It's empowering because teachers see that changes in their behavior lead to students feeling more safe and respected and students learning more in class. After all, most teachers want their students to do well and want to interrupt anything they're doing that's holding students back. Once we release ourselves from having to prove we're bias-free, we can focus our energy on making our practice increasingly fair.

As with any improvement work, less is more. We can't tackle every area at once. Just as a tennis coach would never lead a novice tennis player through every stroke and nuance of the game during the first lesson, we're not going to address all the areas where unconscious racial bias thrives at once. Strategic leaders bring resources and focus to bear on one topic at a time and build a habit of reflective inquiry. Then they're able to engage teachers in authentically leading the improvement process.

In this chapter, we'll examine where bias may show up in a schoolwide campus climate—notably in relationships between students and staff and in peer-to-peer relationships—and what we as educators can do about it. In chapter 7, we'll zero in on these relationships inside the classroom. In chapter 8, we'll examine how bias might appear in academics and how to reduce it to bring about improvement. We'll start with a discussion of what we mean by climate in general and racial climate in particular.

EXAMINE SCHOOL AND CLASSROOM CLIMATE

As most educators know, climate refers to the culture of the school or classroom. Is it overcast and gloomy? Are students tense or on guard due to an atmosphere of fear or intimidation? Or is there warmth, support, appreciation, and welcome for students, individually and collectively? Classroom and school climate is determined by the interactions among teachers, students, and administrators. The tone we set, what we celebrate, and what we condone all contribute to climate. It's crucial to student success. School systems contribute to the school-level climate, while individual teacher actions create the classroom climate.

Ample research connects school and classroom climate to academic success. A 1997 study confirmed the link between school climate and academics. The report explained that students who experience a positive school climate exhibit higher rates of academic achievement and motivation to learn, and have better school attendance and study habits.[1] In a classroom environment study of fourth and fifth graders, researchers found that classroom climate (student satisfaction, levels of student-to-student cohesion, perceived competition) was correlated to student academic self-efficacy.[2] In this study, the researchers found that the more students indicated greater satisfaction with the classroom, especially in the area of belonging, the more students were willing to engage in academic tasks. Climate matters for student learning.

What Is Racial Climate?

Leaders generally agree that attending to a school's climate is important work, yet few receive guidance on how to deal with the *racial* climate of their school communities. Researchers define campus racial climate as how often students experience or witness intentional or unintentional acts of discrimination or prejudice.[3] They find damaging effects on the academic achievement of students of color who indicate being subject to or witnessing high levels of perceived discrimination.[4] Racial climate may show up in interactions among students, interactions between students and teachers, participation levels in school activities, and levels of trust or suspicion between teachers and students and among students.

Many leaders may assume that their schools have a positive racial climate simply because there is an absence of blatant racism. We talked to a principal who said he saw black students and white students interacting during class transitions and so was confident—relieved—that his school was free of racism. However, schools don't have to be overtly racist to be hostile environments for students of color. Students of color may experience high levels of perceived discrimination multiple times a day, throughout the school day, without the knowledge of teachers or administrators. Some students may not be aware that the feeling of marginalization they're experiencing is the outcome of racial bias, but the impact of exclusion is no less detrimental. Since we're all equally susceptible to unconscious bias, any of us as educators may be contributing to a negative racial climate in small or large ways. As a result, on a daily basis, students of color may feel less welcomed in asking for help, less cared for, and less supported and encouraged than their white peers. Committing to students' success in school requires committing to a positive racial climate for all students.

Racial Climate Affects All Students

When we as educators think about how unconscious racial bias plays out in our schools, we often assume students of color alone feel the impact. However, white students are harmed as well. Bystanders or witnesses to biased behavior—even and especially when subtle—absorb the impact as well. Every time we assign a disproportionate percentage of students of color to lower-level classes and assign them a less experienced teacher, fail to address underrepresentation of students of color in sports or clubs, or punish students of color for behavior that white students engage in without consequence, we teach students, through our action or inaction, that giving preference to white people is acceptable, normal, and expected. So while black students experience daily exclusion or marginalization, white students experience a normalization of bias. While students of color are most directly affected, monitoring and reducing the impact of unconscious racial bias serves all students.

For example, during his time as a high school principal, Tracey consistently reminded faculty and staff to "address the misbehavior, not the student," by which he meant they should remember to respond in a consistent tone and demeanor to all students regardless of race. Tracey shared his learnings about his unfair treatment of black and brown students in the hallway as an example of how a student's race can alter the ways we respond.

Students experience racial climate at two levels: in individual classrooms and on a schoolwide level. To improve a school's racial climate, we need to investigate and address potential bias at both levels. We as leaders need to examine schoolwide systems that reinforce racial biases, and we need to support teachers in examining their individual routines and behaviors as well.

Next, we will explore how leaders support their school communities to address racial climate at both levels through examining student-student interactions, teacher-student interactions, student participation levels, and discipline.

SUPPORT STUDENT-TEACHER INTERACTIONS SCHOOLWIDE

Ferguson and Ramsdell, in a 2001 study on teaching effectiveness, as measured by student perceptions, found that students who feel more connected to teachers tend to perform better academically. Specifically, in this study, when students indicated that they felt "cared for" and "respected" by their teacher, they were more likely to exhibit signs of academic success. The measures of care and success in this study were fairly simple. Students rated teachers on a numerical scale in response to these two prompts: (1) "My teacher makes me feel that s/he really cares about me"; and (2) "My teacher wants us to share our thoughts."[5]

How can a school examine the quality of teacher-student interactions? How can we hold ourselves accountable for demonstrating respect and caring for *all* of our students? Unfortunately, our gut instincts won't be a reliable measure. Most of us are likely to feel that we generally have good relationships with our students. We exchange greetings and pleasantries, we don't experience friction, we joke about the football game, and we bake cookies for students' birthdays. However, while these acts may feel caring to us, what matters is what feels caring to students. Ferguson and Ramsdell's study went beyond these kinds of interactions to understand interactions that students experienced as genuine caring and respect for themselves as individuals. If we want to conduct a serious inquiry into the possible effects of our bias, we need to understand a student's experience more deeply and systematically. We need to determine whether we are more effective at showing respect and care for white students than students of color.

Audit Relationships

One fall when Tracey was a principal, during an afternoon professional development session, he led teachers in an activity to explore teacher-student relationships. He was concerned about the number of students of color who were frequently absent from school as well as the disproportionate percentage of students of color assigned to in-school suspension. To prepare for the professional development session, he wrote the name of every student in the school on a sticky note and placed the notes on the cafeteria walls. Once all teachers arrived at the professional development session, he asked the group to scan the walls and collect the names of the students they felt they had a close relationship with. After the teachers finished collecting their names, he asked the group to scan those left on the wall for similarities. While the students left on the wall were racially diverse, students of color were clearly overrepresented.

Tracey used this newly uncovered knowledge to launch a one-on-one mentoring program in the school, specifically aimed at improving the campus racial climate by helping teachers forge relationships with more students of color. Helping teachers clearly see the differential treatment of students of color increased some teachers' willingness to voluntarily mentor one or two of the students of color whose names remained on the wall. Several months after the mentoring program began, Tracey reported to teachers a significant improvement in attendance and in-school suspension numbers of students of color, especially those who were assigned a one-on-one mentor.

This sticky-note activity has many variations. A leader might have teachers place dots on a list of students with whom they have a connection. This also indicates patterns among the students with whom many people have relationships. Who are they? Is the staff better at forming meaningful relationships with white students than with students of color? What would staff need to do to ensure all students believe at least one adult cares for and respects them? An audit can make student-teacher interactions visible. It can focus the spotlight on that child who comes to school each day without feeling cared for or respected. Teachers who want the best for their students can develop a more systematic approach to cultivating relationships based on genuine caring and respect.

Sarah has implemented a version of this activity with elementary school teachers, where class lists are shorter (although not for specialist teachers, who could benefit more from the sticky-note exercise). Next to each name on a class list, teachers write something they know about that student's interests outside school. After going through the list, teachers put a star next to the names of students who are aware that the teacher knows this thing about them. In other words, they have made a connection with the student about this outside-school activity or interest. Then teachers reflect on any patterns. Were there any patterns along lines of race? Was it easier to come up with personal information about students whose backgrounds were similar to the teacher's?

Another self-check is to invite educators, at the end of each day, to write down the names of those students they've had a meaningful, positive interaction with that day. Patterns will start to appear. Some students' names repeatedly never come up. Perhaps these are the students teachers had only negative interactions with. Other students simply are invisible. Sometimes the patterns reveal racial disparities. Could we be manifesting an unconscious preference for a particular racial group? For most of us, this is not something we're used to thinking about, so we might have to face our own resistance to this thought. However, discovering how our unconscious may be leading to unequal treatment of students can also be empowering. A kindergarten teacher told us that when he did a similar exercise with a group of teachers, in each case the student who was last on everyone's list was a black girl. He said the insight was a powerful one for him and made him return to his classroom with a determination to know all of his students and, in particular, the black girls well. Recognizing the impact of our biases can spur action. Establishing a deliberate system like Tracey's mentoring system or, in elementary schools, a list to track what we know about each student would help to ensure no child is deprived of a caring, respectful connection to an adult in the building. While these forms of data collection are not neutral—they're filtered through our recollections and thus not objective—they can reveal useful patterns.

Collect Information on Other Relationships

A great way to learn about students' experience of the classroom and school climate is to ask them. Do students feel their teachers care for and respect them? Do they feel their teachers listen and welcome their feedback? Do students feel they are treated fairly? These and other questions are good fodder for racial climate surveys. Increasing numbers of student surveys are available online for the full range of grades. Researcher Ron Ferguson's well-known Tripod survey is available in formats appropriate for kindergarteners through twelfth grade. Some schools devise their own.

A middle school staff created a survey of teacher-student interactions that all students take twice a year. School leaders reserve time so that as soon as the results are available, teachers meet in teams to analyze the feedback and create action plans to address any concerns. Several months later, after the second round of the survey, teachers and administrators can see if their plans have had an impact.

Many of the surveys we've seen omit a crucial factor, however. They neglect to ask students to identify their race. Without this information, the data may hide important racial disparities in students' experiences. For example, if 85 percent of students say they feel their teachers respect them, schools may perceive this as a fairly encouraging number. However, if the school is racially diverse and the remaining 15 percent who don't feel respected are all Latino/a students, then the picture is quite different—and concerning. Surfacing this information is critical to addressing it. In order to discover our potential racial blind spots, our tools cannot be race neutral; disaggregating data helps surface important information.

Tracey realized the importance of recording racial identifiers when collecting climate data at his school. When he first began looking at school climate data collected at a middle school, he noticed a peculiar trend in students' responses to two particular prompts: "The school rules are fair" and "My teachers care about me and treat me fairly." As Tracey reviewed several consecutive years of school climate data results, he noticed that every year, the responses to these two questions were relatively positive in the sixth grade, dipped significantly in the seventh grade, and then rose slightly in the eighth grade. After examining these trends and comparing them to the significant rise in suspension rates of all students, even more so among students of color in the seventh grade, Tracey began to wonder if the dip in the responses to the two prompts were disproportionately coming from students of color. However, since the school had decided to keep all surveys anonymous, Traccy was not able to use the data to examine how school climate affected specific groups of students.

One reason to normalize talking about race is to prepare educators to dis-aggregate and discuss data by racial identifiers. In the previous example, if Tracey had the opportunity to administer the survey again, he would add race and gender identifiers. The reason for the identifiers is to allow for disag-gregation by categories such as black girls, white boys, and so on. By creating discrete categories, leaders are able to see a fuller picture of the experience of specific student groups that would otherwise be hidden within nondescript data. Also, when developing racial categories, it is best to avoid overly broad categories, such as "people of color," since these types of categories can obscure the experiences of specific racial groups.

What about schools that are racially homogeneous? How might survey data help teachers and administrators seek out and address areas where they are manifesting their unconscious biases? In these cases, disaggregating sur-vey data won't reveal differences in the experiences of different racial groups. However, with a student population that is 100 percent students of color, a survey question like "I feel my race is respected at this school [or in this class-room]" can provide important information. In addition, comparing responses to a question about race from one classroom to another or one grade to another can surface useful data about where teachers may unconsciously be commu-nicating disrespect to a racial group.

In addition to formal surveys, teachers can always informally survey their students. As leaders, we can schedule time for teams of teachers to come up with informal exit tickets or other consistent, ongoing formats for monitor-ing students' experiences in the school and classroom climate. Teams can col-laborate to examine the data and brainstorm possible responses if the results show racial disparities.

Ask Students About Their Racialized Experiences

Surveys can also include questions specifically about students' racialized expe-riences in school. After all, if we're problem seekers, this is the information we are looking for, and we know that, in our society, there's no such thing as a race-neutral setting. A typical survey may ask students to rate how safe they feel at school on a scale of 1 to 5. In order to use this question to mea-sure racial climate, this item can be modified to read, "On a scale of 1 to 5, I feel students of my race are safe at school." Or "On a scale of 1 to 5, I feel students of other races are safe at school." These two revised questions elicit very different responses than the race-blind survey question. Learning about how both white students and students of color perceive their school's climate reveals important information as well. Specifically, the questions give us insight into how often students are witnessing racially biased behaviors. The disaggregated data will also tell us if the experiences of the white students at a school are different from the experiences of students of color.

Some other questions we've found helpful for school leaders and teachers when investigating student experiences of schoolwide racial climate are: "Are there times, occasions, classes, clubs, or sports where we see consistent racial segregation or under- or overrepresentation of students of color? If so, how might we survey students to investigate for possible signs of unconscious racial bias? How can we develop a plan to measure campus racial climate that takes into account the views of students, teachers, and parents? Regardless of student body demographics (i.e., racially heterogeneous, all African American, all white, all Latino/a, all Asian), how can we measure campus racial climate so that we understand how unconscious racial bias functions at our school?"

Listen to Students' Criticisms

Students often provide teachers with rich data about their classroom experience. However, often the data don't come in the form of "Teacher, I feel X, because of Y; therefore I need Z." Most often, from kindergarten through high school, the data come in the form of behaviors, off-the-cuff comments, or expressed emotions.

Teachers and administrators simply do not have enough time during the school day to treat every student comment as a starting point for investigation. However, we as educators can try to be more alert to comments indicating a racial disparity we aren't aware of. In particular, there's one form of student feedback data that is almost always worth investigating further—student criticism. Especially when we're seeking to uncover our unconscious racial biases, we need to be ready to hear things about our behavior that we just can't know on our own and that we don't want to believe is true.

One of the biggest triggers for teachers is when students call them racist. This can also be an invaluable source of information. Tracey remembers a biology teacher bursting into the principal's office, referral in hand, furious that a student had called him racist. Several other students had agreed that they felt he was "kinda racist." When Tracey asked if the teacher had talked to any of the students about this, the teacher was shocked and asked, "What for?" Tracey replied, "To find out what they mean."

This reminds us of a valuable suggestion from educator Elizabeth Denevi. She asks, "What if being called 'racist' is the beginning and not the end of the conversation?"[6] Denevi sympathizes with teachers and administrators who see this accusation as the "Scarlett R."[7] Few things feel as hurtful to a white person striving to do right by students. The word stings when students direct it toward educators of color as well. However, when we accept that our racial biases are unconscious, we have to accept that we have blind spots. In this context, feedback from students, which may feel offensive, is ultimately a gift.

For example, during his time as a high school principal, Tracey had assigned a black student an in-school suspension for being late to class multiple times over the course of a week. The student called him an "Uncle Tom" as he exited his office. Knowing the student was using this term to tell Tracey that he thought he was a "sellout" or was being unfair to black students, Tracey called the student back into his office. Once Tracey allowed the student to calm down, instead of scolding him for calling him an Uncle Tom, Tracey asked the student why he felt the need to use that term. The conversation that ensued was very eye-opening. To the student, by assigning him school suspension, Tracey was supporting some of the teachers in the unfair treatment of students of color. In his view, the write-up from his teacher for being tardy to class was discriminatory because he would consistently see white kids arrive to class after him but not receive write-ups or an office referral. Whether or not this was true, the student believed it and therefore saw Tracey, another black male, as a supporter of the teacher's discriminatory actions toward him, a black, male student. Tracey followed up on the student's concern after he walked him to the school suspension.

Too often, when students give unsolicited, critical feedback, the response is to (1) explain to the student why his or her observation is incorrect, (2) become defensive and deny the accusation, or (3) seek to punish the student for the unwanted feedback. These responses help no one. We as educators may have a host of reasons we know the student is wrong. One may be that we feel the student is simply trying to be hurtful, and sometimes that may be the case. However, when we assume this is always the case or when we don't investigate, even when we're certain this is the case, we take several significant risks. First, we risk not learning something we really need to hear. Second, we risk continuing to traumatize a student in ways we do not know. When we're told we're racist or otherwise receive feedback about potential racial bias, we have to receive it openly.

If the situation feels too charged, we may want to buy time ("I will talk about this with you later"). It's also helpful to process our feelings and initial response with a trusted colleague until we can listen sincerely and truly consider the student's point of view. If we're truly committed to having a positive impact on student learning, we need to be open to hearing about the impact of our actions and what that feels like for students.

INVESTIGATE STUDENT-TO-STUDENT INTERACTIONS

In addition to looking at staff-student interactions, it's important to explore the racial dynamics in peer-to-peer relationships. How do students in a school and in classrooms interact with each other? Do students hang out exclusively with students of the same race? Have these groups formed naturally or are there broader patterns of racial segregation playing out? How do the different racial groups decide who is accepted into their groups? How do they interact with other racial groups? These questions are all important to consider when examining the racial climate in schools.

Examine Student Participation

A key area to investigate for the impact of potential bias is student participation in various school and classroom activities. Participation can range from trying out for the school musical to raising a hand during class discussion to volunteering to feed the fish. As educators, we want to make sure our school and classroom climate encourages and doesn't inhibit student participation.

At the middle school where Tracey was assistant principal, several after-school teachers wondered why black and Latino/a students did not enroll in after-school activities at the same rates as white students. At one point, Tracey presented data about the disproportionate failure rates of black and Latino/a students at the school. After the presentation, three teachers approached Tracey to express their concerns that students in these groups opted to take the bus home instead of staying for after-school homework help or extracurricular programming. These teachers had approached several students of color who were not performing well academically and invited them to stay after school for extra help, but most of them had chosen to opt out. In order to learn more, Tracey audited the rates of participation in all after-school activities (i.e., clubs, athletics, tutoring) by race. After examining the compiled data, Tracey found that while black and Latino/a students comprised about 20 percent of the total student body, these students represented only 1 percent of participants in after-school activities.

To investigate these trends further, Tracey's leadership team administered a schoolwide survey to students about their attitudes toward after-school activities. Through the survey, the school discovered that a majority of black and Latino/a students, regardless of income level, wanted to participate in after-school activities. They chose not to primarily for three reasons: (1) they felt that if they elected to participate, they would be the only student of color in the club; (2) they felt that because they would be the only student of color in the club, they would not have any friends; and (3) they felt that their teachers did not care if they stayed after school for extra help.

Before administering the survey, most of the concerned after-school teachers believed their black and brown students did not participate in after-school academic programs for three different reasons: (1) they did not care enough about their grades; (2) they did not have anyone at home who cared enough to make them stay after school; (3) they had younger brothers and sisters to care for at home immediately after school. However, the survey showed that for the majority of students, none of these assumptions proved to be true. While well meaning, these assumptions were inaccurate and rooted in preconceived notions about black and Latino/a students, not in the reality of these students' experiences.

After reviewing the survey results, teachers developed two strategies to increase after-school participation. First, the leadership team assigned each teacher a small friend-group of black and/or Latino/a students to reach out to, mentor, and enroll in after-school activities. Second, the leadership team monitored after-school attendance weekly and had each teacher check in with his or her assigned friend-group during the school day to make sure the group planned to stay after school. This strategy yielded an increase from 1 percent participation of black and Latino/a students in after-school activities to 54 percent after one quarter. Moreover, the increased relationship building and academic supports led to improved academic performance for many of the participating students. In addition, the few students who had had high rates of suspension and detention improved their behavior.

Like Tracey's staff, we may learn a great deal by examining participation rates in school activities, such as extracurricular sports and clubs, enrollment in honors and AP courses, athletics, open house, and parent-teacher nights. What aspects of school might students of color feel is not for them? What assumptions might we be making when we see low participation rates of students of color? How might adult actions and beliefs be contributing to low participation rates?

When we as leaders and teachers examine trends of underenrollment or nonparticipation, it's helpful to question our assumptions. As happened at Tracey's school, adult perceptions and beliefs might inhibit teachers from seeing that they can make a huge difference.

CHAPTER 7

Examining Instruction and Classroom Climate

Once we as leaders have identified patterns in schoolwide relationships that shape a school's racial climate, we can dig deeper by observing classroom climate—how teachers interact with the students in their classrooms, and how peers interact with one another. These relationships are expressed both in teaching and learning activities and in classroom management patterns, often the source of racial disparities in disciplinary referrals. While the student surveys discussed in the previous chapter may yield some information about classroom climate, typically it's best to follow up with direct observation of classroom practice.

Focused observations are a powerful tool for uncovering biases we don't know we have. Leaders can support teachers to observe in each other's classrooms or videotape a lesson to investigate specific questions about teacher-student interactions: "What are my patterns in calling on students to answer questions? Who participates in class discussion and who doesn't? Who participates in side conversations and who doesn't, and which of these students do I notice? Do some students tend not to raise their hands at all? Do some students call out without penalty, while others receive redirection?"

In her advice to coaches, coaching expert Elena Aguilar recommends explicitly tracking student-teacher interactions to monitor for possible biases during lessons.[1] She describes a tracking tool that lays out the data to collect in columns across the top of the page: time, gender, race/ethnicity, transcript. When teachers invite her to, or in circumstances when she thinks the data are necessary to alert the teacher to an unknown problem, Aguilar writes a quick description of what the teacher said in each interaction. She and the teacher can then analyze the interactions to see if there are patterns. When they find patterns, she can help the teacher develop systems to override the bias that's creating the patterns. Systems might include a method for calling on students fairly, ensuring all students receive encouragement, and monitoring who is calling out. She and the teacher can then use the observation tool again to see if the system they devised is addressing the specific pattern they identified.

While coaching a highly skilled new math teacher, Tracey discovered another way that unconscious racial bias can manifest itself: in body language. Shortly after the new teacher began teaching, she requested that Tracey observe her more frequently than required and give her feedback to improve her practice. The teacher's enthusiasm for teaching was infectious, and Tracey was eager to support her. During one observation, Tracey noticed that all the students of color in her algebra class sat in the two rows along the left wall, while the white students occupied the four other rows. He also noticed that the teacher would position her body during the lesson toward the white students, leaving the two rows of students of color relegated to her periphery. During the lesson, Tracey tracked the number of students who raised their hands to participate in the class discussion as well as the number who were actually called on.

During their post-observation conference, Tracey shared his observations with the teacher. Not a single student of color had raised his or her hand or was called on during the entire lesson. The white students, on the other hand, had raised their hands and participated over thirty times, with some students participating more than once. The teacher was surprised. She thanked Tracey for the observations, asked for advice, and requested that he observe her again the next day. When he returned to the same class for the observation the next day, the teacher had taken his advice and positioned herself on the other side of the room facing the entire class. Students of color raised their hands more than on the previous day and she called on them more often. When the teacher was able to make eye contact with the students and see their faces, their participation increased.

This teacher had been completely unaware of how her physical position in class had cut off students of color. Without intending to, her body language unconsciously prioritized the learning of white students over students of color.

This incident didn't reduce Tracey's respect for the new teacher. He didn't sort her into the "bad, racist" category because her actions seemed influenced by unconscious racial biases. He continued to be impressed with her pedagogy and believed in her intentions to help all her students excel. Simultaneously, in his classroom observations, he continued to collect data on ways teachers' unconscious biases might unintentionally but harmfully exclude students of color. When we or others collect observational data, we can surface unconscious prioritizing and allow teachers to take action to address it.

How many of us may unintentionally be doing something similar to what this math teacher was doing? Given the universality of unconscious racial bias, probably most of us as educators send subtle but persistent messages that white students are more worthy of our attention and more favored in intellectual discourse. The disturbing reality is that whether through verbal or nonverbal communication, students receive messages about their value and worth on a minute-to-minute basis during classroom instruction. These messages, delivered unconsciously, daily, over time, have a profound effect on students. The good news is that we can do something about it. Knowledge of our biases gives us the power to reduce their impact. Observational data can point us to concrete behaviors to change and monitor in order to be the fair and encouraging educators we strive to be.

In the fast-paced classroom setting, teachers are not always aware of how their actions and words are affecting students. Questions to consider when exploring how unconscious racial bias manifests itself in the classroom are: "Who are my go-to students for answers during direct instruction? Which students do I expect will need a little more help to answer a question correctly? Which students tend not to raise their hands at all? Which students tend to raise their hands frequently? Are there students who call out without penalty, but others who are penalized for the same behavior? Do I provide my students the opportunity to give me feedback about how they feel about me?"

OBSERVE WHO SEEKS ACADEMIC HELP

As teachers, we have all taught students who hesitated to ask for academic help, even when they were thoroughly confused or completely lost. We have also probably noticed that when given the option, some students decided to approach a friend for help rather than a teacher. In a study of high school students, researchers found that students valued friendliness, trustworthiness, and the ability of the listener to empathize when selecting whom to reach out to for help.[2] This same study found that students tended to avoid approaching a teacher for help because, instead of empathizing with the student, teachers tended to solely focus on solving the problem. These findings highlight the role relationships play in students' behavior in seeking help.

If we tend to establish relationships more easily with certain groups of students, then they are likely to be the ones who approach us for academic help more often. As this pattern develops during the school year, students we have not formed relationships with may likewise develop a pattern of not seeking help, which may compound over time, making them less and less likely to seek help as the year progresses. So while we may feel that we're making ourselves available to all students or we may have an explicit open-door policy for students to ask for help, our ability to form authentic relationships with students may play a bigger role than we think in a student's willingness to approach us.

The good news is that students' comfort and willingness to approach us for help is well within our control. When examining trends in help-seeking behavior, we can ask ourselves questions such as: "Which students tend to seek academic help most often? Are there racial differences between students who do and do not seek help? How are my relationships with the students who struggle, but consistently do not seek help? When students who rarely reach out for help finally do, do I try and empathize with them and build a relationship or do I tend to just problem solve? For the students who do seek help frequently, are my interactions different with them than other students who seek help less frequently?"

INVESTIGATE ASSUMPTIONS ABOUT STUDENT PARTICIPATION

Who gets called on in class is a common, important thing to monitor. However, it's also useful to observe who raises their hand to begin with. Which students volunteer to participate in class in this way? If no students raised their hands to respond to a teacher's question, educators would notice. However, if a subgroup never raised their hands, would educators notice as much? When are we concerned about lack of participation from a student and when do we let it slide? Would we be more likely to be concerned if it is white students who are reticent and less likely to seek a solution if students of color repeatedly do not participate?

At Sarah's school, a teacher made a discovery. While tutoring a first-grade black student in reading, she was delighted to realize that he understood the story better than she had thought. She asked the child why he never raised his hand in class to talk about the stories they read together. He explained that his family had told him to be quiet in school and not disturb the teacher. He had interpreted this as not raising his hand. This child's family was from Ethiopia, and when teachers investigated, they discovered that other Ethiopian students at the school were similarly silent during class discussions. The teaching team decided that teachers would speak to this boy and other students to explain that raising hands in class was something they wanted students to do and that it helped their learning. While change didn't happen overnight, the teachers were persistent in explaining their expectations and, over time, reported much more participation from the Ethiopian students.

Sarah and her staff wondered if unconscious bias had influenced their complacency with this and the silence of other black students in class. Were they quicker to assume the student wasn't capable rather than wonder what might be inhibiting him from participating? Auditing student participation in class is an important step. Soliciting input from students is a crucial follow-up.

Listen to Students' Feedback

One often neglected area to examine within individual classrooms is how students are experiencing their peer-to-peer interactions. It can be useful to track the partnering behavior of students for signs of intragroup racial bias and discrimination. In some cases, students may seek out racial affinity groups for positive reasons. However, we can't assume this is always the case. When white students consistently work together more often than with students of color, exclusion may be taking place. Students of color may pair up in response to exclusion from their white peers. Again, surveys or exit tickets that allow students to respond to specific prompts ("Students of my race are treated fairly during group work") can help us determine if there are patterns of racial exclusion happening in student groups.

We as educators also need to be alert to informal feedback from students. After attending a workshop on unconscious racial bias, a teacher told Sarah that he had a new insight about something a student once said to him. The student asked to switch groups for science class and explained that the boys in his group were being mean. The teacher moved the boy and explained to Sarah that he'd always regretted that he didn't address the mean behavior of the boys. After the workshop, however, he realized that he also may have missed an important moment to address racial bias in his classroom. The boy who switched groups was Latino; all the other boys were white. At the time, he hadn't paid attention to race in the situation. Now he realized that his Latino student may have been experiencing a hostile racial climate. Without investigating, the teacher didn't know whether this was evidence of a more systematic problem he could have addressed. Perhaps his Latino student was striving to learn in an environment that may have been explicitly hostile to his racial background. In addition, if the white students' bullying was racialized, the teacher had allowed it to continue, further impacting the racial climate in the classroom and at the school. This teacher explained that going forward, he will be more alert to possible racial bias in his classroom. In addition to addressing bullying, he may need to teach his students about the lies of racism and how they—like adults—can look out for ways it may be affecting their behaviors.

In a parallel example, Tracey remembers a student who regularly told him he felt dumb. Tracey just as regularly would refute the child's claim and give some encouragement: "I don't think you are dumb; it's just that it may take more time for you to figure out the word problems . . . and that's okay." After a few months of this pattern, the student asked to speak with Tracey privately. He explained that he felt dumb because during times when he was required to collaborate within a group, his peers would insist on rechecking all the answers to the problems he was assigned, but not rechecking anyone else's. Tracey realized that this student's "I feel dumb" comment was data that he had overlooked. Words of affirmation had not addressed the root problem. If he'd approached this student's concern as a starting point for investigation and if he had been curious about whether race might be playing a role, Tracey might have been able to address the situation earlier.

When considering investigating classroom racial climate, specifically peer working relationships, processing of student feedback, and assignment of classroom consequences, we find these questions helpful: "Are the groups in my classroom typically racially segregated? If the groups are racially integrated, do I have a sense of how the students of color are experiencing these groups?

Do I collect data on my classroom racial climate? What sources about my classroom racial climate could I collect data on? Are there racial discrepancies in my classroom consequences? If I do not know, how can I examine data to find out or begin a process of collecting data?"

EXAMINE APPROACHES TO CLASSROOM DISCIPLINE

Another factor that contributes to both school and classroom climate is the way we as educators respond to misbehavior. Fair treatment promotes a feeling of safety and respect; unfair treatment leads to wariness, suspicion, and an overall negative climate. As would be true for any of us, when students perceive a discipline system as unfair (and when that system is, in fact, unfair), their trust in the people administering the system erodes and a negative climate forms. In fundamental ways, our approach to discipline affects students' ability to learn.

It's impossible to address racial disparities in student discipline without understanding our society's criminalization of black lives. A proactive step we can take as leaders is to help ourselves and our staff understand the effect this criminalization has on our unconscious reactions and split-second decisions and, therefore, the impact this has on students. The phenomenon of criminalizing blackness is not new, but it is gaining more widespread attention in the age of social media. As one example, the hashtag #WhileBlack documents countless situations when black people were engaged in everyday activities and white people responded with suspicion and fear. For example, white people called the police in the following instances: a black resident was at his building's private pool, a black college student ate lunch alone in a common room, a black congressional representative walked door to door to meet her constituents, a black graduate student fell asleep in her dorm library, two black men waited for a colleague at a Starbucks, and many more incidents.[3] As referenced in chapter 1, research has shown that people of all races are more likely to associate black people with crime than white people.

One telling study showed pictures of people holding an object in their hands. On average, when the person in the picture was black, participants in the study were more likely to believe they saw a gun in the person's hand than they were with pictures of white people holding an object.[4] As with so many examples of unconscious racial bias, these reactions were very quick—milliseconds, the same amount of time it takes many of us to decide to reprimand a student or send a student to the office. These unconscious racial biases—absorbed involuntarily like breathing in smog—influence countless decisions in schools, from how we interpret a student's reply when we ask him or her a question to how we respond when we see a student laughing in the hallway to how we perceive a student who asks for a pencil. They force us to ask, "What if the overrepresentation of black and brown students in the school office has more to do with adults' biases than children's behaviors?"

Most educators are familiar with statistics showing racial disparities in school suspension rates.[5] Many educators assume that these statistics demonstrate that black students misbehave more than white students. However, a growing body of research shows that the disparities are more likely tied to adult behaviors and perceptions than to disparities in student behavior. For example, in the Stanford study cited in chapter 1, teachers were more likely to label a student as a troublemaker, find his or her behavior irritating, and recommend a harsher consequence if the student had a name that sounded black.[6] While none of us wants to accept it, our perceptions of students are not neutral. Our biases inevitably influence how we respond to student behavior.

Bias Starts with How We Interpret Student Behaviors

In a 2002 study, researchers found that referrals originating in the classroom make up a vast majority of the gaps between black and white student suspensions, far more than differences in administrative responses once the referral has reached the office.[7] According to the research, "Although boys were slightly more likely than girls to be suspended once referred to the office, measures of administrative response were almost identical for white and black students . . . administrative decisions regarding school suspension did not appear to be the primary source of disciplinary disproportionality."[8] These researchers concluded that the discrepancy in school suspension was more directly correlated to racially disproportionate filing of discipline referrals by classroom teachers. Moreover, they also found "no evidence that racial disparities in school punishment could be explained by higher rates of African American misbehavior."[9] These findings highlight a well-identified trend in contemporary research whereby students of color, especially black students, are subject to harsher punishments, especially in the classroom, than their white peers for engaging in the same behaviors.

In other research into the racial disparities in disciplinary action, researchers found that the majority of office referrals were for highly subjective categories of misbehavior such as "insubordination," "defiance," and "disrespect." The unconscious biases of educators can lead to completely different outcomes for groups of students of different races. A group of black students speaking loudly together in the hall may be sent to the office, while a group of white students' loud behavior may be interpreted as normal teenage behavior that merits a reminder to be quiet in the halls or no response at all. Tracey's experience when he found himself reprimanding black students congregating in the hallway and ignoring white students exhibiting the same behavior is an example.

This phenomenon of interpreting the same behavior differently for black and white students is vividly explained in a detailed 2016 study of racial disparities at a high school in the Midwest.[10] In this study, researchers Amanda Lewis and John Diamond conducted hundreds of hours of interviews and observations at a racially integrated, well-respected high school. They found that students, teachers, and administrators at the school were all aware that the educators applied the rules differently to black students than they did white students. Lewis and Diamond explain that this was not because staff members were overtly racist. On the contrary, the researchers stated, "for the most part we did not find evidence of explicit racism or intentional favoritism"; rather, they heard from staff "an expressed philosophy to close the achievement gap and an almost universally espoused commitment to equity."[11] This was a school with unquestionably good intentions. Yet, the staff's approach to discipline was rife with racial bias.

In this school, teachers, administrators, and students of all races explained that black students were regularly disciplined for infractions regarding dress code, cursing, permission to use the bathroom, and use of the hallway pass, whereas white students were given a second chance or, more often, their infractions were ignored. As one administrator expressed, "All kids do something wrong. Why do the blacks have to be the ones that always have to be disciplined and the white kids are supposed to be understood?" Other teachers and administrators described a similar dynamic. For example, one teacher said, "There are certain groups of kids who are labeled and who tend to get written up more. You know, you can have six white kids in a hallway being loud, and a teacher will walk by and see that and say, 'Move along.' Okay? You can have six black children in the hallway being loud, and they call security. Okay?" Lewis and Diamond show over and over that student behaviors were the same, but adult interpretation and response to the behaviors favored leniency for white students and viewed students of color with suspicion.[12]

Most teachers would doubt this to be true about themselves and their school. Learning about the research helps people see the problem; recognizing that this bias happens in schools committed to racial equity may help people accept that they're not immune. Most importantly, this knowledge empowers educators to do something about it and therefore improve outcomes for students.

Increasing Consistency in Responses to Misbehavior

A common response to inconsistencies in our behavior is, not surprisingly, an attempt to be more consistent. Certainly, consistency can help. As Lewis and Diamond conclude from their study, "Where there is discretion, there will be discrimination."[13] Reducing the amount of discretion in a system can't eradicate discrimination, but it can reduce it. One tool that helps is an external checklist or flowchart.

Other institutions striving to address unconscious biases may have lessons to teach educators. When doctors at Johns Hopkins Hospital uncovered a gender bias in their diagnosis of blood clot risk factors, they mandated the use of a standardized checklist. All doctors had to ask a series of questions and essentially follow a flowchart for decision making and diagnosis. The checklist didn't remove judgment; it improved it. It ensured that everyone went through a minimum of steps and didn't skip any because unconscious biases led them to make assumptions. As a result, the disparities in diagnoses virtually disappeared.[14] In a similar way, Google and other tech companies use a structured interview template in order to reduce the amount of discretion in interviews and thereby reduce the amount of unconscious bias that creeps into unstructured conversations. Checklists and flowcharts help to ensure greater consistency in areas that are susceptible to bias.

At Sarah's school, teachers concerned about inconsistencies in discipline across the school created a guidance document called "Pathways for Dealing with Inappropriate Behavior." The document includes a flowchart of gradu-ated steps of discipline with reminders at each step to communicate with fami-lies, connect with students, and collaborate with administrators. As a result, fewer teachers send students to the office for minor infractions; they agreed to follow the steps on the flowchart. Such structures reduce the likelihood of an individual teacher or administrator skipping over multiple pathways in a moment of tension and going straight to an office referral or suspension.

When Tracey began as an administrator at his high school, he saw dis-parities in when teachers sent a student to the office as well as how adminis-trators responded. Black students were sent to the office for minor offenses. Once students were in the office, the pattern was often to verbally reprimand white students or call home and to give detentions and suspensions to black students.

To increase consistency and fairness, Tracey established a standardized school-discipline protocol. Decisions to suspend or assign detention were no longer simply a matter of personal judgment, often in the heat of the moment. Instead, teachers and administrators followed a matrix of responses, outlined in a shared handbook. As a result, students could no longer be sent to the office for not having a pencil or get detention for not doing their homework. Student detentions, suspensions, and expulsions decreased. Standardizing systems for determining disciplinary responses reduces discretion and, there-fore, discrimination. Often people consider standardized rules as tools for students. In this context, standardized rules posted in a classroom or hallway are an essential aid for *the educators*, so that we can hold ourselves account-able for following the school and classroom management systems and inter-preting behaviors with fidelity.

When Tracey standardized his hallway monitoring, he saw an improvement in all student behavior. Each day he reminded himself to correct behaviors and not students. After a few weeks of consistently and uniformly enforc-ing the "no congregating in the halls" rule during passing time, his school experienced a significant drop in the number of referrals that teachers made regarding students of color being "insubordinate" in the hallways. Tracey was certain that the increased uniform enforcement and decrease in student refer-rals were connected. The more students of color saw teachers treating everyone equally and fairly, the more willing they became to comply with the rules. Tracey noticed an interesting change. Previously, he passed by white students to redirect students of color. When he began addressing every group congregating in the hallways, very often the groups farther from him would see him coming and disperse before he even arrived. White students as well as students of color recognized that the rules applied to everyone.

Clear management systems at the school and classroom levels can help increase consistency; however, they are not enough to completely eliminate the impact of unconscious racial bias. After all, in all of the examples we've shared about ourselves and other educators exhibiting biased behavior, *we thought we were being fair.* That's what makes addressing this so challenging. Unconscious bias creeps in as we interpret student behavior. We make decisions quickly and under stressful conditions, when we're most susceptible to bias influencing our actions. Since we can't trust our instincts, collecting data from external sources becomes an essential tool.

Monitoring and Managing Discipline Data

Schools are required to keep data about suspensions, but many don't keep records of other disciplinary action. Whether we're looking at office referrals, names teachers write on the board, kids who sit on the bench at recess, detention, suspension, or whatever other form of discipline is used, a wide range of data will help us investigate basic questions: "Are there racial differences between consequences assigned to students of color and white students for the same behaviors? Is there an overrepresentation of any racial group? Is there a trend in particular behaviors that lead to a particular consequence? Is there a correlation between the number of students of color in a particular class and the number of referrals for that class? Do we perceive a 'good kid/bad kid' categorization that falls along racial lines?"

One objective method for assessing racial bias in classroom discipline practices is a consequence and behavior audit. An audit of student behaviors and related consequences can help to uncover racially biased treatment of students. A behavior-consequence audit involves an observer tracking on- and off-task behaviors, the race of the student, and response of the teacher. What this process often reveals is (1) teachers do not address every off-task behavior, (2) which types of off-task behaviors they are more likely to address, (3) which off-task behaviors they are likely not to address, and (4) which behaviors they tolerate and do not tolerate, depending on the student.

For example, during one classroom observation, Tracey collected data about how rules were enforced differently for white students and students of color in the same classroom. During an independent work time, he noticed that white students repeatedly left their seats and walked up to the teacher's desk to ask for and receive help. At the same time, he noticed that students of color stayed in their seats and raised their hands to ask for help.

Tracey was confident that this teacher did not have a rule that only white children could leave their seats without permission; yet, somehow this had become a classroom norm. Later, Tracey asked the teacher about kids leaving their seats to ask for her help. The teacher explained that she had a rule that no one could leave their seat without permission and that students who had a question should stay seated and raise their hand. When Tracey described what he'd observed, the teacher was surprised. The data he shared helped her realize that her behaviors did not reflect her intention. On subsequent observations, she enforced the rule more consistently. Setting aside the particulars of this teacher's pedagogy, this is an example of how data can help us surface unconscious biases and address them.

At one school, administrators sought to shed new light on potential biases. They collected the numbers of merits and demerits assigned to students and whether the students were failing in any classes. They disaggregated these data by race, gender, and special education status and then compared each group's percentage of the overall student population to their proportion of merits, demerits, and failed classes. They then shared these data with teachers. Teachers could see that Latina girls received 33 percent fewer demerits and 10 percent fewer merits than would be expected based on their percent of the school population. The percent of Latina girls failing class was also 39 percent higher than would be expected given their percentage of the overall school population. Latina girls were slipping under the radar. At the same time, black boys received 92 percent more demerits and 13 percent more merits than expected, and 72 percent of them were failing classes. The administrator said that the data produced valuable reflection and conversation about race, gender, ability, and bias. Calculating the risk factor for students made the racial disparities plain and enabled teachers to see that their teaching practices were not serving all students equally well. Teachers reported that the process prompted them to do more research to understand students' experience better so they could figure out more accurately how to address the disparities.[15]

Anticipating and Addressing Resistance

As a result of reducing discretion and introducing systems to increase fairness in our behaviors, we'll begin to see shifts in patterns at our schools. When the patterns are different from what we're used to, they can be disconcerting. When we're used to racially disparate patterns in disciplinary action, fairness can feel jarring and even uncomfortable.

Research has consistently shown that students of color tend to receive harsher consequences than their white counterparts for similar behaviors.[16] So when students of color stop receiving harsher consequences and white students stop receiving greater amounts of leniency, some educators can be disoriented. More than a new policy is needed to change beliefs about who should be punished and who deserves a second chance. It's challenging when the beliefs are conscious, and more challenging when the beliefs are unconscious. If this were a technical fix, then changing the school policy would be sufficient to produce our desired outcomes. However, policies that require us to act counter to our learned instincts require changing mindsets, a much more difficult process. We should expect resistance.

After Tracey's school standardized the school-discipline protocol, it saw a significant decrease in student detentions, suspensions, and expulsions. Tracey and his administrative team supported teachers in developing consistent classroom rules, consequences, and procedures for classroom management. Likewise, administrators standardized and made public the systems and structures for consistent student consequences. These efforts to squeeze as much unconscious bias from the system were successful. However, some teachers found the changes uncomfortable.

After the school began following a more consistent approach to assigning suspensions, a teacher noticed a white student she knew being suspended, something she hadn't expected. Even after she learned that the student had punched another student in the face, the teacher remarked to Tracey with surprise and dismay, "Wow, these new rules and procedures are just sending anybody to in-school suspension, even the good kids." This exchange between Tracey and the teacher exemplifies how bias continues to persevere in schools. Whatever your view of appropriate disciplinary action and whether and when suspensions are an option, we can all agree that when students misbehave, they deserve to be treated fairly. The students we label "good kids," who tend more often to be white, too often receive second chances when misbehaving, while the students we label "bad kids," who often tend to be black and brown, get punished for the same behaviors. Sometimes these beliefs come from a place where teachers truly believe that "bad kids" need to be punished more harshly because they just don't learn, or that "good kids" shouldn't be punished at all because they will change their behavior through discussion and reflection.

As leaders, we can be alert to this resistance by listening to the ways we and our staff talk about students. Do we hear ourselves or others refer to students of color as "those kids" or "the other kids"? This type of language can be a key indicator that a racially biased good kids/bad kids dynamic is forming in a school. Discovering that this language has taken hold can feel jarring. School leaders may find themselves asking, "How did we get here?" or "How come I did not notice this before now?" While these questions are valid and worth exploring, we won't make progress by simply admiring the problem. Instead, we can ask ourselves, "What's my first step on the road to recovery?" and "What resources and support do I need to turn the tide?"

Tracey witnessed a veteran teacher struggle with his school's new approach to discipline that treated all students equally. About a month after launching the system of school discipline that reduced teacher discretion in assigning consequences, this teacher came to Tracey demanding that the school create a separate system that would assign more harsh consequences for the students she referred to as the "bad kids." She was upset that within the new, standardized system, "good kids" were getting in trouble more often, while the "bad kids" weren't getting the harsh punishments they needed. This teacher was so distraught about the new system that she broke into tears when she talked about one of her favorite students receiving in-school suspension for cutting class three times. At the same time, she was angry that another student only received after-school detention for calling another student a "fat ass" during class. This teacher had clearly come to believe that some kids were exempt from the rules.

These examples may seem extreme to some readers, but they were not unusual at Tracey's school and many other schools we've visited. For all of us, this mindset of good kids and bad kids is likely more rooted in our minds than we think. We know because harsher punishment for black students is pervasive. As we've described earlier, the impacts are felt not just by those who are subject to the discipline but by bystanders who witness the unfair treatment as well. When Tracey enforced greater consistency in sending kids in the hallways to class, the white students were surprised to be reprimanded. They even looked confused, as if wondering why they were now being held to rules that previously they had been exempt from. We can understand that confused look. While students of color had learned that they would receive harsher consequences than their white peers, white students had become accustomed to leniency or exemption from the rules. In this way, schools reproduce the unconscious biases we're trying to root out.

WHAT'S THE SOLUTION?

Readers may be eager to get to some solutions. Once we identify racial discrepancies in school and classroom practices, what should we do? One simple answer is that after you identify a racial discrepancy, your follow-up action plan will probably need to involve the three following steps: (1) design and implement clear systems or structures, (2) determine objective criteria, and (3) increase collaboration. Examples of all of the above are folded into chapters six through eight.

These three steps are attractive because they can be checked off a list. "Did I create a *system* to ensure I learn about each child's personal interests? Do we have clear *criteria* for how a child gets sent to the office? Do teachers *collaborate* with colleagues when they are determining a consequence for what they perceive to be misbehavior?" However, there's also a danger in recommending these three steps. It would be easy to think that once we've checked a step off our list, we have ensured fair treatment of all students. It's not that simple.

Creating a system—or setting up criteria or increasing collaboration—will be helpful, but it will not be sufficient to ensure that black and brown students receive equal treatment. We also need to accept that unconscious bias will continually creep into the school day, by continually creeping into our thinking. We address it not by creating systems alone, but by increasingly shedding defensiveness and adopting a mindset of inquiry.

Accepting that we are continually influenced by unconscious biases requires replacing the racist/nonracist binary mindset with an open, nondefensive mindset of inquiry. This work is not simple. Prioritizing students' experiences over adults' self-image involves long-term self-examination, reflection, and genuine inquiry.

This is why we do not describe specific technical practices that all schools should implement. Will teachers increase fairness if they use a particular system to assign classroom jobs? Probably. However, that's the starting point, not the end point. We hope teachers and administrators will see the goal as ongoing examination of our impact, not just dutifully instituting specific procedures.

When technical steps are presented as the work to do, they may be more dangerous than helpful. They may distract leaders from going deeper. It's always easier to check off something on a list than to question our beliefs and actions. Uprooting racism is an enormous task. Liberation will not come through surface changes. As a friend warns, "Don't think that a few technical steps will eliminate the danger you pose to the kids you care about."

We create more equitable outcomes when we establish student outcomes as the most important guide in determining what practices we implement. *What is our impact on students of color? How will we find out?* Once we identify bias in our existing systems, we'll develop structures, criteria, and collaborative processes to reduce it. Through this ongoing inquiry process, we'll build a culture of continual investigation and growth to address the racial bias that lives in our schools and ourselves.

School and classroom climate are not the only areas to investigate, however. School communities also need to examine their overall approach to academics. Are the systems and structures that explicitly support academic learning set up to serve all students equally well? In chapter eight, we suggest a variety of ways to explore this question.

CHAPTER 8

Addressing Unconscious Bias in Academics

How does unconscious racial bias show up in academics in schools? This is new territory for most educators, since few learned about this topic in teacher or administrator preparation programs. Unconscious racial bias shows up in some obvious ways, as in expectations for students, and also in less obvious ways, such as the books displayed in the library. Once again, we advocate adopting an inquiry approach to develop the habit of continually asking ourselves as educators, "What might we be missing? How can we learn more about our students' experience of our academic program?"

The goal is to create a school culture where we continually seek to uncover how bias is interfering with our aspirations and then come up with systems and structures to eradicate or reduce the impact of our bias. In order to arrive at the right solutions, leaders cultivate a community where it's normal to ask, "What assumptions do we need to question? How might our biases be holding back black and brown students?" Collecting data through observations and audits provides the raw material for inquiry. Then teachers and administrators work together to determine how to change practices to reduce the impact of bias on students. We suggest three main areas for investigation: representation, expectations, and selection.

REPRESENTATION MATTERS

On the Walls

As a middle school student, Tracey noticed that in his classrooms, the only pictures were of white people. Posters on the walls were either text or white people. Pictures on teachers' desks were of the teachers' all-white families. Tracey remembers talking about this with other black students; they collectively wished they saw pictures of people who looked like them in their classrooms. Tracey and his friends shared this wish with their principal, who responded by pointing to the pictures in his own office as evidence that there was no ill-will intended: "See? All the pictures on my desk are of white people, too. It's just that those are the people in my family." And he encouraged the students not to worry about it.

This principal didn't say anything that wasn't true. However, he missed an opportunity to better understand Tracey and his friends' perspective and consider how it might expand his own racialized view of the world. The solution isn't for teachers to remove the pictures of their family, or insert random pictures of Martin Luther King Jr. next to Aunt Susie. There are plenty of ways for teachers and schools to ensure that students see themselves reflected in positive and powerful ways. As one small example, when Kofi Annan was appointed Secretary-General of the United Nations, Sarah explained his role and hung his picture in her fifth-grade classroom. For months afterward, a group of black boys regularly pointed to the poster of the black man, sometimes greeting Annan as they entered or exited the classroom. One boy explained proudly, "Kofi Annan is basically the president of the world. He's my man." It was striking how much affirmation her students drew from this picture.

When Teachers College professor Christopher Emdin interviewed students of color at their schools, he noticed that their responses differed based on their surroundings. In classrooms that were more traditional, with nothing or just pictures of white people on the walls, students were less forthcoming. However, when the same students were interviewed in classrooms that reflected the students' identities—through pictures of the students themselves, a wall painted with blackboard paint that students wrote on, posters of hip-hop artists whom the students admired—the students appeared more comfortable and spoke more extensively in interviews.[1]

In another school, a Native American student felt excluded by the pictures on the wall of his counselor's office for a slightly different reason. During a meeting, the counselor referenced a Hollywood image on the wall. The picture depicted a man wearing a loincloth and feather as an inspirational poster. The student later angrily told a visiting ethnographer, "That picture isn't us!" and refused to return to the counselor's office for guidance. (Based on the counselor's comments to the student, this may have protected him from further insult and misguided career advice.)[2]

Throughout the daily experience of school, representation affects student learning. How are we ensuring that all children, families, and faculty members feel their experience is valued and reflected in school? Equally important, how do we ensure that all children—and particularly white children—gain views into experiences and perspectives different from their own?

In the Curriculum

This guideline extends beyond what we hang on the wall to the assignments we provide. A brief activity in graduate school was a stark reminder to Tracey of how even a simple conversation prompt can communicate a strong sense of exclusion. A few of his classmates led an icebreaker activity in which they invited their peers to get to know each other by responding to the prompt, "How did your ancestors come to America?" The sense of exclusion was immediate for Tracey and probably the other students of color in the class. While most of the white students shared stories about how their ancestors arrived on US shores as immigrants from European countries, the students of color and especially black students had a very different story that was not so lighthearted. Their stories were about their ancestors who had arrived in shackles as slaves or about slavery making it impossible for them to trace their lineage back that far. Rather than increase a sense of connection, this activity increased the feeling of exclusion for students of color who were not able to experience the activity in a lighthearted way.

While some readers may see this assignment as an obvious mistake, examples like this are common in schools across the country. They don't usually come from a place of malice but rather ignorance. Most white people are unconscious of their racialized experience and the fact that it's not an experience everyone shares. Adrienne Rich described the experience most children of color have in school: "When someone with the authority of a teacher, say, describes the world and you are not in it, there is a moment of psychic disequilibrium, as if you looked into a mirror and saw nothing."[3] As school leaders, we can help our staff ask themselves the question, "When our students of color move through their day in school, how do they see themselves represented?" When we provide time and support for teachers to explore their racialized experience, we allow white teachers to see that their lived experience is not universal. Then they can apply this insight to their teaching and regularly ask themselves, "How do I ensure the experiences of black and brown students are viewed as normal and valued?"

Leaders can also introduce a metaphor we've found many educators appreciate and use in their teaching. The concept of "windows and mirrors" helps educators evaluate their practice regarding representation. Educator Emily Style introduced this conceptual tool to describe what all teaching should include.[4] Windows provide a view into life experiences different from our own. Mirrors reflect our life experiences. All children—and adults—need to experience windows and mirrors when they learn. As educators, we have the power to do this.

While much of a school's curriculum content is determined by standards outside the school walls, there's still considerable discretion in what content teachers bring into the classroom and, importantly, how they teach it. The following text from a poster on the wall of a classroom provides useful guidance for both students and teachers:

> Always ask yourself:
> Who writes the stories?
> Who benefits from the stories?
> Who is missing from the stories?

One form of data to collect is simply to audit the curriculum to see how it portrays people of color. Is the only mention of people of color in the context of oppression and struggle? Are positive and varied images of people of color present in textbooks, read-alouds, and reading group assignments? When Tracey was a teacher, he discovered that his textbooks included pictures of only white people. So he looked for every opportunity to use black- and

Latino/a-sounding names in his examples in class, on worksheets, and on tests and quizzes. He didn't want his curriculum to communicate on a daily basis that math (or reading or science) is only for white people. He wanted his students of color to see themselves throughout the curriculum.

Sarah recently saw a simple example of mirrors for students of color in the library at the Capital City Public Charter School. As in every library, most books were shelved with their spines outward, with a few books on every shelf positioned so their covers showed. Throughout the library, across genres, every single book with the cover displayed was about people of color (and no, it wasn't Black History Month).

Now wait a minute, some people may be saying. Doesn't that just replicate the problem for white students? Shouldn't they see themselves in the mirror as well? Absolutely. And they do. The experiences and reflections of white people are affirmed in countless ways in our society in movies, books, news media, advertising, and more. This librarian may simply have been ensuring, in her own way, that every time children of color came to the library, they would get a similar blast of simple affirmation: *You belong here. Your experiences and history and ideas are valuable and worthy of study.*

Schools can audit their curriculum and general instructional materials. When looking at what to include in a library, a curriculum's scope and sequence, the books we choose for read-alouds and reading assignments, and what we display on bulletin boards and walls, we need to ask ourselves, "Does this material take into account the experiences of people of all races or does it center and normalize only the experiences of white people?" We can start by simply counting references to people of color. List all the books we assign students to read. How many include people of color as protagonists? Examine the last month of assignments. Do they affirm the experiences of people of color or do they assume a white experience is universal? Auditing a curriculum's anchor texts requires examining not just whether people of color are represented but how. As one organization's curriculum auditing tool asks, "Does this material show self-efficacy by showing people of color helping themselves rather than requiring white people to intervene to improve circumstances?"[5]

In the overall picture of school, the content of an icebreaker activity or the names used in a math textbook may seem insignificant. However, these seemingly minor details have the potential to harm the psychological well-being of students of color as well as white students. For students of color, the constant exposure to a white-centric curriculum and images sends the daily message that white is the norm—the standard—and being of color is different from normal or less than the standard. For white students, the pervasive experience of not seeing people of color in the curriculum reinforces the misconception that the white experience is universal and worthy of examination and that the experiences of people of color are of less interest and value than whites.

EXPECTATIONS MATTER

One of the most fundamental and pernicious ways that unconscious racial bias operates is through lowering academic standards for students of color. This creates a vicious cycle. With lower expectations, students of color learn less. As a consequence, when they're assessed, they do not meet the standards. Based on these assessment results, students of color are perceived to be less capable, so educators lower their expectations. The cycle repeats, and students of color fall further and further behind.

Even though most of us think we have high expectations, we may not actually believe that black and brown students will end up as future engineers, doctors, teachers, or artists. In one meeting of administrators who worked at schools with almost 100 percent black and brown students, school leaders discussed the importance of practicing clear classroom procedures. One administrator explained the benefit by saying, "When that kid grows up, he won't have to search for his work boots or his tools; he'll know exactly where he put them." No one said a word to contradict the school leader. Her assumption that this child would end up in a job involving manual labor belied her other stated belief that she had high expectations for all students. How would that assumption influence the kinds of questions she expected teachers to ask students during science lab or a discussion of expository writing?

We know enough by now to realize that intentions aren't enough. If we want to be sure that our actions align with our intentions, we need to take the extra step to investigate the outcomes of our practice. Where should we investigate? Low expectations can show up in practices and policies from an individual teacher's grading to a schoolwide scheduling policy. The following examples do not constitute a comprehensive list of places to investigate, but they provide an entry point.

Evaluating Student Work

It's hard to be absolutely fair in assessing students' work, no matter what their racial identity. Our opinions about students and their capacity inevitably come to bear on our assessments: *We've told Christina countless times to show her work, so when she omits it, we may take off the maximum number of points. However, when Isaac forgets to do the same thing, we just write a reminder to "show your work" since we know it was a temporary slip-up for this typically high-performing student.* Knowledge of our students influences any assessment of their work.

A common pitfall in schools is teachers lowering their academic standards for black and brown students out of a feeling of pity. Teachers may assume their black and brown students come from low-income families or experience challenging lives outside of school. They relax their standards for these students because they feel sorry for them. This is problematic for several reasons.

First, while it's true that many of the students experiencing poverty may be students of color, this is not true for all students of color. Second, lowering standards is a disservice to any student because we're lowering the quality of that student's education and consequently his or her opportunities in life. We may also be fostering a sense of learned helplessness. Third, when faced with a student who is, in fact, experiencing tough out-of-school circumstances, the appropriate step is to check in with the student or her family to see if she needs support. We take this step to ensure the child has the resources to be successful in school, as we simultaneously provide this child with the level of rigor we expect of all students.

We can help to monitor our unconscious biases by establishing some checks and balances in our feedback on student work. One way to ensure we consistently hold high standards is by periodically monitoring our feedback or evaluations of a student's competence or quality of work.

One monitoring method is to implement a system of blind grading. In this method, teachers pass around a numbered sheet of paper before giving a quiz or test and ask each student to write his or her name next to a number. Students then write the same number at the top of their test instead of writing their name. After collecting and grading each test, the teacher can match the name with the number. Even with electronic submission, teachers can devise a drop-box system that ensures anonymity of submitted student work.

Another method of checking bias is for teachers who do not share the same students to periodically swap student papers for grading. This could be a great opportunity not only to check grading fairness and consistency, but also to engage in conversation about what specific aspects of the student work may be leading to biased grading. A few reflection questions teachers may want to consider when implementing blind grading are: Did any student or groups of students score better or worse than I expected? If there are differences in expected and actual grades, what could be the cause? How might unconscious biases play a role in these differences?

Evaluating Expectations for Learning

Another way to monitor student learning is by observing teacher-student inter-actions. The staff at one school was investigating low levels of analytic think-ing, which had been identified as an area of low achievement on standardized tests. They conducted instructional rounds to learn more about the types of questions they were using with students. After educators visited classrooms, wrote down exactly what they heard, and came together to compare notes, they found a pattern. The data revealed that students of color were asked questions with low levels of cognitive demand, whereas white students in general were asked questions that required more depth of thinking. Rather than trying to explain away this finding, the teachers saw it as an opportunity to understand how bias might be unconsciously affecting their interactions with students.

Another practice is to have a colleague observe and audit a class discussion or work period. Similar to the audit of teacher-student interaction to assess classroom climate, this audit specifically examines the quality and academic rigor of the feedback and responses teachers give to students during class dis-cussions and work times. Observers (or teachers reviewing videotape of their class) can use the same observation sheet that collects data on student race and gender and the type of interaction that's occurring (question, follow-up probe, feedback) and transcribe the wording of the interaction. This then allows teachers to examine whether their high expectations for students are coming through in their academic interactions with them in class.

A recent TNTP report confirmed the need to continually examine the aca-demic expectations of students. Researchers studied five large districts serv-ing primarily students of color and found that the majority of assignments teachers gave to students were below grade level. A compelling graph extrapolates from the data to show that of the 180 classroom hours spent in each core subject each year, students spent only 47 hours on grade-level appropriate assignments.[6]

Signaling Expectations for Students

A 2003 study conducted in North Carolina found that, compared to white students, African American students across multiple school districts were disproportionately assigned to novice teachers.[7] Similarly, a more recent study conducted in 2012 found that more academically and behaviorally challenging classes, especially those with a greater percentage of African American students, were assigned to novice teachers across all types of schools.[8] These two studies highlight the vital need to examine how leaders schedule classes, organize teachers, and assign students. School leaders who honestly examine expectations for students may change the way they distribute human capital in schools.

As anyone who has been a first-year teacher knows, teaching involves a steep learning curve. While there are always exceptions, novice teachers are generally not as skilled as their more experienced peers. Yet, middle and high school department chairs and administrators regularly assign novice teachers to teach the students who are least proficient in the content area. These beginning and remedial courses are considered more difficult to teach. A common practice in schools is to assign students in beginning or remedial courses— those who most need expert instruction in order to help them catch up to their peers—to receive instruction from those with the smallest repertoire of teaching strategies. This system has developed as a way of rewarding teachers for their experience. Because these classes are often those with disproportionately high numbers of students of color, the system also prioritizes teacher choice over the learning needs of students of color. Underlying these teacher assignment procedures may be an unconscious racial bias that the white students are more likely to succeed and are more worthy of teacher attention and, correspondingly, that the black and brown students are less able and have less inherent academic potential.

This phenomenon occurs in elementary schools, too. In K–5 settings that have the benefit of student teachers or assistant teachers, teachers often assign these staff members to work with the lowest-performing students. When the students who are struggling the hardest are also kids of color, this practice may reflect the same unconscious racial bias as in the middle and high school example above. A teacher who makes such assignments may feel that a small group of struggling students is a better setting in which to practice teaching, that lower-level instruction is easier for an inexperienced or noncertified teacher to handle, or that high-level learners require more sophisticated teaching that a student teacher is not yet prepared to deliver. Upon closer examination, however, most of us would find these assumptions flawed. In order to catch up to grade level, students who struggle the most need the teacher with the greatest pedagogical expertise. Denying them that expertise may signal a deep-rooted belief that they are not capable of catching up to their peers.

At the schools where Sarah was principal, most teachers had student teachers or assistant teachers. She sent a reminder to teachers each year that the lowest-performing students (the majority of whom were students of color) always needed to be taught by the adult in the classroom with the greatest level of teaching experience. While there were always teachers at her school who didn't need this reminder; there were also always teachers who did.

One year, Tracey set up a system to monitor data about teacher assignments at his school, which tracked students into either Honors and Advanced Placement classes or "standard-level" classes. He pulled two different class schedules from each grade from each track and looked at the level of experience of the teachers for each sample schedule. Students in the standard-level track were assigned, on average, two novice teachers for their core classes (math, science, social studies, English), while the vast majority of students assigned to the Honors and AP track never worked with a novice teacher. This meant that, in total over the course of four years in high school, students on the standard-level track were exposed to an average of eight novice teachers, whereas students in the Honors and AP track rarely if ever were taught by a new teacher. No one explicitly designed the school schedule with the intention of putting students of color at a disadvantage. Yet, since the vast majority of students of color at Tracey's school were enrolled in standard-level courses, this is exactly what was happening.

After discussing the issue at length with nearly every department in the building, Tracey and his leadership team devised a schedule that distributed teachers throughout all course levels, so that novice teachers were equally represented across all classes. This adjustment in teacher-student assignment, in conjunction with several other initiatives, helped improve student academic achievement, lower absenteeism, and decrease the incidence of student drop-outs in the ninth grade. However, the change was not easy to implement and did not come without considerable challenges.

One significant, unintended consequence of this policy change was that multiple veteran teachers at Tracey's school resigned, retired early, or trans-ferred to a different school because they did not want to teach lower-level classes. They felt they had "put in their time" with the standard-level classes and deserved the privilege of teaching Honors classes. Thus, the number of novice teachers on staff grew in the first year of full, schoolwide implemen-tation. Despite the very real loss of veteran teachers, Tracey and his leader-ship team held steady and went through with the change because they were determined that the high school would no longer subscribe to a practice that disproportionately and negatively impacted students of color. However, it's important to note that it was not all smooth sailing.

Decisions like these are not easy. It is no small task to schedule a large stu-dent body, organize classes, and simultaneously honor teacher preferences, while making sure not to disproportionately disadvantage any group of stu-dents. We know what it's like as school leaders spending long hours play-ing master-schedule *Tetris* every year, only to have to go back to square one when enrollment fluctuations or unseen circumstances require a change to a course or teacher's assignment. Real-world constraints simply do not always allow for equal distribution of experienced and novice teachers. In addition, school culture can be tough to change, especially when experienced and effec-tive teachers are willing to resign if a decision does not meet their approval. However, at the end of the day, the questions remain: Do I believe black and brown students are capable of excelling academically? Do my school policies of teacher assignment align with that belief?

To investigate these questions, leaders might develop a monitoring system. For example, they might start an annual practice of pulling sample sched-ules in the way that Tracey did or color-coding the school schedule for years of teaching or come up with another system for monitoring teacher assign-ments. Tracey encouraged his leadership team to regularly investigate whether there was a disproportionate representation of students of color in a particular class or course level and if this trend had persisted over time. School leaders might ask: What are the practices of teacher assignment at my school and do they demonstrate a belief in all students' ability to succeed or do they indicate an underlying complacency with poor performance for some subgroups of students?

When investigating policies and practices for teacher assignment, school leaders might ask: Is there disproportionate representation of students of color in a particular class or course level? If so, has this trend persisted over time? Is there a culture of assigning experienced teachers to particular classes? If so, does this culture disproportionately negatively affect students of color? What can be done to disrupt the impacts of unconscious racial bias in student-teacher assignment?

SELECTION PROCESSES MATTER

Throughout the school year, students are selected for a variety of things from awards to AP classes to classroom privileges. How students are selected is often an informal process. However, as Lewis and Diamond remind us, "Where there is discretion, there will be discrimination."[9] Leaders can help reduce discrimination in selection processes by auditing them and coming up with systems and criteria to reduce discrimination in the first place. Next, we review just a few examples of selection processes.

Selection for Special Jobs

Every day, educators select students to help collect papers, pass out assignments, or take a note to the office. Sometimes, these are assigned jobs that rotate. Other times, they are spur-of-the-moment decisions that involve determining who will be the most likely to run an errand without dilly-dallying. On the surface, these decisions appear to be based on logic. However, as with many decisions—particularly those made quickly—unconscious racial bias may influence us more than we think.

When we mentally run through our class list or scan faces to choose a reliable candidate, we may unconsciously show a preference for white students. Without deliberately monitoring these choices, these unconscious preferences for seemingly small classroom privileges may persist day after day. What may seem minor when looked at as a single occurrence can feel like consistent exclusion to a child who is never selected.

It would be easy to underestimate the impact of this daily event. We remind ourselves to consider the situation from a single student's perspective. Constant exposure to a teacher's unconscious preference for white students can take a toll on a student's motivation, self-esteem, and feelings of acceptance. Most students, especially younger ones, may not be able to pinpoint the source of these feelings or describe them to the teacher. Instead, they may communicate their feelings of frustration and resentment by shutting down, acting out, or misbehaving. Understanding this may help us see how our repeated, unconscious behavior as adults can contribute to a child's frustration and alienation in school. Recognizing our role also means we can change it.

Selection for Honors or Advanced Placement

On a larger scale, students are regularly selected for honors and various forms of recognition. For example, at many schools, students are selected for "leader of the month" or for character or achievement awards. In most cases, there isn't a highly formalized selection process; rather, teachers meet to discuss who is right for the recognition. Once again, this situation includes considerable discretion, so it is likely to contain much discrimination as well.

An African American visitor witnessed an end-of-year school celebration that raised red flags for her. During the ceremony, school administrators awarded many students for their academic achievements as well as their progress and performance in a range of character skills that the school valued. Student after student rose to get awards for things like persistence, honesty, gratitude, and generosity. Not a single student was black, even though black students made up 40 percent of the school's population. This visitor shared her concern with the school's teachers, who were shocked when they looked at the overall data. What had seemed glaringly obvious to the visitor and likely many of the students in the school had gone unnoticed by the staff. After this, the staff came up with a more systematic way to determine awards, including clearly spelled-out criteria and a scoring system rather than informal conversations.

Similarly, schools often rely on teacher recommendations to determine who is assigned to Advanced Placement classes. In his school, Tracey immediately introduced two policies to reduce discretion in this process: student placement depended on grades and not teacher recommendation; teachers could not turn away a student who had been assigned to an AP class. At Capital City, after examining data about racial disparities in student assignment, a science teacher changed the process she uses for AP Physics assignments. She said that when she first started making the assignments, "I always thought about kids and just had a gut instinct and wasn't basing it on data at all. Then I realized this was incredibly biased." Now, in the process she uses, students have to show that they are able to complete a math problem representing the type of math they will need to use in the AP class. They also take a survey that asks about their career interests, and the teacher uses this to recommend students who may be borderline in their math ability. The survey also allows her to have conversations with students about other preparation they will need to complete to pursue their dream career.

Audits can help leaders see if there are racial disparities in the selection process. Clear criteria for privileges and awards reduce the influence of biases. Determining the criteria ahead of time also helps. A few questions we find helpful to consider are: Are there patterns in the students selected for special privileges and/or awards? Are students from one racial group more or less represented than other racial groups? Are certain students selected very often, while others are not? If there is an established system for selecting students, does everyone have an equal opportunity to be selected?

Selection extends to class grades as well, since many teachers include a range of factors in their grading systems. Questions to consider when examining student passing rates in academics are: Are there patterns along racial lines among students who fail to progress to the next grade level? If so, how should the school begin investigating where racial bias may be at play? Are there certain teachers who fail more students of color than others? Are there racial discrepancies among students who are enrolled in remedial or credit-recovery programs? Is there racial bias in the assignment of students to remedial courses?

Persistent exposure to racial bias has negative effects on children of all races. This bias is particularly pernicious when it occurs in schools, where students come to learn in a safe and supportive environment. When students of color do not see themselves represented, they develop the sense that people like them do not fit the image of who is important, normal, or valued. When white students learn within an environment that overwhelmingly represents and affirms their racial identity, to the exclusion of people of other races, they begin to internalize racial bias, even at early ages. As educators, we have the power to either reinforce or interrupt this repeating, reinforcing cycle. Examining curricular materials, teacher expectations, and student placement are just some of the ways to uncover and address how racial bias is promoted in schools.

CHAPTER 9

Reframing the Problem

Examining data is a crucial step in the process of uncovering bias in order to address it. However, it would be a mistake to assume that by putting the data in front of teachers, the problem will be self-evident. Analyzing data doesn't happen in a vacuum. All of us are susceptible to drawing false conclusions, especially when the data line up with biases we've been taught as truth. Our interpretations can reveal more about what our unconscious biases tell us than about what the data actually tell us. As leaders foster a culture of inquiry, it's important to foster a sense of teacher responsibility for outcomes at the same time. Otherwise, examining data will simply reinforce biases and won't lead to changes in teacher practice.

For example, when Diane, a white primary-grade teacher, began working at Sarah's school, she was startled to see the way teachers discussed students' reading assessments. Before a meeting early in the year, her colleagues had disaggregated the formative reading assessment data by race. They planned to discuss the patterns they saw in the results, which showed a disproportionate number of black students reading below grade level and remaining stuck there. As the teachers gathered for their meeting, Diane protested that her colleagues were racist. She said she was tired of educators blaming black students for their low academic performance. Didn't they know that these students worked hard and had a lot to cope with at home? Their parents did their best, but they had multiple jobs and couldn't always be available for their children.

They were hard-working, lovely children, and she wished people would stop indicating they were failures by just focusing on their low scores. She refused to be part of the meeting.

Her bewildered colleagues shared this incident with Sarah, who was then prepared when Diane came into her office later that day to register her complaint. Sarah explained that the teaching team disaggregated the data by race because they felt the results reflected on teacher performance, and they were determined to learn what they could do differently so their black students learned more. After hearing this, the teacher who had been righteously fuming seemed honestly stunned. She'd never considered this as a possible perspective. The teachers, Sarah explained, believed that it was their job to ensure that all students were at or above grade level, so if some students weren't there yet, it indicated that the teachers had not yet been successful. Their plan was to investigate the gaps and come up with a plan to close them. Sarah had work to do to support Diane in taking responsibility for student results.

Like many educators—teachers and administrators alike—Diane couldn't see racial disparities in achievement as anything but a reflection of student capacity. In her view, it was unfortunate that black students were below grade level, but it was just the way things were. She had compassion for her black students, but it was clear she viewed their low achievement as outside her control.

Would teachers and administrators have the same view if all the failing students were white? Before we as educators examine any performance data, we need to be rooted in the foundational premise that all students *can meet or exceed grade-level standards*. If we believe—consciously or unconsciously—that black and brown children are less capable, then we'll see their test results and other outcome data as an indictment of their capacity, not ours. In contrast, if we start with the assumption that all children are equally capable, then we will see disparities as reflections of the conditions around those children. Along the way, we may also realize how profoundly radical this assumption is within our culture. As leaders, we have significant agency in shaping how staff members view data and how much responsibility they take for the results of their teaching. We have the power to frame the problem in ways that foster commitment rather than complaint, and responsibility rather than blame.[1]

BIAS INFLUENCES HOW WE INTERPRET DATA

Consider a scenario in which all the children assigned to sit on the right side of the classroom did more poorly on a series of assessments than the children on the left side of the classroom. When examining these results, we would never leap to the assumption that the children seated on the right side are less capable. That doesn't match what we know is true about students. We would immediately assume that the study indicates something else is going on in that classroom, something external to the students. Based on the data, we would likely conclude that something in the conditions of that classroom is inhibiting the kids on the right side from succeeding.

We wouldn't think for a second that students who sit on the right side are inherently less capable. There is no difference in capacity between children who sit on one or the other side of a classroom. But what if all the children on the right side of the room were black? Would we be more likely to feel that it reflects something about the students themselves rather than the conditions in which they learn—conditions that we as adults establish and maintain?

Sarah faced this question when she spoke with a black parent at her school who was also an education professor. The parent told Sarah about a recent study showing that middle- and upper-class black students at high-performing private schools received lower grades on average than their white peers. Sarah's reaction was telling. Why would this parent want to tell her about a study confirming that black students were less capable? This seemed to be a devastating piece of research. She'd always believed that all children could achieve at high levels, and here was this research disproving it. Fortunately, in that moment of disequilibrium, Sarah asked the parent how she was making sense of the research.

The professor replied that it was depressing to see that racial bias was alive and well, even when you were controlling for socioeconomic class. You couldn't make the common claim that the differences were really about income, so it was a clear indication to her of racial bias. This explanation wasn't what Sarah expected. She kept listening.

The professor went on to explain that she wasn't questioning the actual grades. She didn't doubt that students' math scores were lower or essays were less well written. She was questioning the conditions—the instruction—that led to that outcome. Could it be that teachers didn't expect their black students to do better and so didn't feel alarmed when they got Bs or Cs? Perhaps teachers didn't tell the students to come for extra help or require a rewrite of a paper. They may not have followed up with black students about late papers, sloppy work, or incomplete homework in the way they followed up with white students. Teachers may not have called these students' parents to alert them to a concern. (Subsequent research of a highly respected affluent public high school documents these very patterns of differential treatment.[2])

For this professor, the study results were personal. She had to be vigilant in watching her black son's progress in school. She couldn't trust that educators would automatically have high expectations for her child, even if they thought they did.

The contrast with Sarah's interpretation of the data was striking. The professor started from the conviction that all black students are inherently capable of high performance. She never for a moment questioned the black students' ability to achieve at high levels. As a consequence, when she read this research, she identified several other areas she would want to investigate. Sarah had simply accepted the results as a description of students' capabilities. She never questioned the conditions surrounding the students.

Where do our convictions lie? Are we certain that black and brown students are inherently capable? Or are we more confident that the conditions surrounding them are inherently trustworthy? Could it be that all the black students in that highly selective high school were academically less capable? That's one possibility. However, in a society shaped so significantly by unconscious racial bias, we can't take racially disparate outcomes at face value. We have to assume a need to explore further to understand the conditions surrounding these outcomes.

DO A ROOT CAUSE ANALYSIS

One strategy for interrupting a deficit approach is root cause analysis. Too often, we think we understand the problem and identify solutions based on this surface diagnosis. If we really want to get at the root, we need to dig deeper.

One administrative team discovered the power of root cause analysis when its members brought a problem to a critical friends' group for advice. The problem was that too many of their students, almost all black students, were being sent to the office for disciplinary referrals. They were committed to reducing this number and had plans to strengthen the teachers' classroom management skills as well as increase the clarity of the school rules and expectations. They invited input from their colleagues by using the "5 Whys" protocol.

Using the protocol, the group brainstormed five consecutive times why the problem existed. During the first brainstorm, the causes were:

- Teachers have no ownership of discipline.
- Students are not engaged in the learning.
- Teachers lack the skills to manage conflict.
- A lot of beginning teachers have weaker management skills.
- Students are performing below grade level so they can't access the curriculum.
- Students are impacted by trauma.
- The rules are unreasonable.
- Expectations around rules are unclear.
- Urgency on growth on state tests makes people feel they can't give time to classroom management.

After the brainstorming, the presenting administrators identified the reason they felt was most relevant to their setting and put that at the top of a blank page. They asked "why" a second time. The next list looked like this:

Students are not engaged in the learning. Why?

- Curriculum isn't relevant.
- Curriculum isn't implemented with fidelity.
- Students don't feel safe or feel comfortable in the classroom.
- Students don't have an entry point.
- Teachers don't present the curriculum in interesting ways.
- Students don't have opportunities to be active.
- Students aren't challenged.
- Students are passive in their learning (because teaching is too teacher-centered).

After the administrators identified "teaching is too teacher-centered" as the most relevant cause in their school, the brainstorming continued. After the fifth round, the possible root causes they had identified looked significantly different from the first round:

We haven't created a vision of a model classroom. Why?

- We don't know what it looks like.
- We haven't established the criteria for that.
- We don't agree on what that looks like.
- We haven't defined cognitive engagement.
- We haven't positioned supervisors to reinforce expectations.
- Supervisors aren't calibrated on expectations.
- We don't have norms or expectations for lesson format.
- We haven't addressed mindsets that stand in the way of pushing for a model classroom.
- Habits of work aren't present in the space.

At the completion of the fifth round, the presenting administrators looked a bit stunned. To their credit, these reflective administrators were willing to leave the protocol process in a different place than they'd started. They shouldered the responsibility to create classrooms that increased student cognitive engagement. Will new teachers need support with classroom management? Of course. However, it became clear during this session that viewing the problem as one of managing student misbehavior was a deficit perspective. Instead, they redefined their work as ensuring that all students have access to engaging, rigorous, and relevant learning and that all administrators understand how to support teachers to get there. This might involve a focus on designing lessons that engage students in giving peer feedback or more use of compelling exemplars or clear connections to issues relevant to students' lives. Administrators who had entered the meeting thinking they needed to improve their staff's ability to teach and enforce rules left the meeting realizing they needed to build teacher capacity to engage and empower students through quality instruction.

BEWARE A DEFICIT VIEW

The process of locating the problem in the student, sometimes referred to as a deficit approach, is a common mindset in schools, even those explicitly committed to social justice and equitable outcomes for all. It can show up in all sorts of well-intentioned practices. This mindset derives from a belief—conscious or unconscious—that some children are inherently less capable. This belief typically drives most of the framing of improvement work. Because the belief is unconscious, it's particularly pernicious and hard to root out. A leadership coach pointed out to Sarah that she was falling into a deficit mode of thinking about student achievement. She described this experience in her book about being a school principal.[3]

Sarah and her staff had fallen into the typical cycle in many American schools. Each time they carefully analyzed the data, they found that the same group of kids—mostly kids of color, mostly low-income, many non-native English speakers—was not making progress. Each time, Sarah and her staff would make plans and hold themselves accountable for providing remediation to help fill the gaps they'd identified in students' learning. Then they'd go through the same cycle again. They were absolutely committed to ensuring all their students reached grade level. However, in their diligent pace around the improvement cycle, they didn't question the fact that the same students were coming up repeatedly. What if the deficits weren't in the students but in the general instruction, the way learning was structured for the whole class? Or the way Sarah as an administrator set up the schedule and expectations?

Sarah and her staff came to realize that they needed to assess some of the basics about classroom instruction and scheduling. Was there enough differentiation from the beginning so that more students could get their needs met during general instruction? Shouldn't the goal be for students to access learning along with their peers rather than repeatedly falling behind and then being pulled from class to catch up? Using this lens, teachers across the grades committed to improving their general reading instruction to meet the needs of the students who had previously had most of their needs met in remedial work. Teachers in the upper grades reserved more time for students to read in class. Teachers in younger grades experimented with a variety of strategies to increase students' reading stamina, including finding high-interest, culturally relevant books. The principal who succeeded Sarah made the wise decision to reallocate resources for before-school reading tutors, who could provide extra support without students missing class time and without teachers being stretched too far.

What Sarah learned from her leadership coach's feedback was that she had been complacent with some students—the same students, the majority of whom were students of color—repeatedly needing remediation. She hadn't questioned the conditions contributing to this outcome. In part, this was because most of the teachers at her school were hard-working and dedicated to their students' success. This pattern persisted because of a combination of faith in teachers' good intentions and respect for their practice combined with an unconscious belief that many children of color would be incapable of performing at grade level. As a result, Sarah's complacency meant she didn't push for further investigation of low student achievement and what staff members (herself included) could do differently to change that. With a barrage of messages communicating low performance of students of color, it's all too easy to locate deficits in the students rather than in our practice as educators. However, as leaders, we can frame problems through a lens of responsibility rather than blame.

FRAME PROBLEMS IN WAYS THAT MATTER

The way we use language frames how we identify responsibility for racial inequities. Unconscious racial biases seep into the way we talk about students, removing teacher responsibility and viewing disparate outcomes as the fault of the students themselves.

For example, in a large high school auditorium recently, teachers gathered from every school in the district for a full-day retreat about "closing racial achievement gaps." The day was billed as honest conversation and confrontation of hard truths. As hundreds of teachers turned their attention to the front of the auditorium, a district administrator welcomed them and began her opening remarks with conviction and a direct, no-nonsense approach: "Our district has a problem: black students."

A black teacher at the meeting quickly looked around at his colleagues to see their reaction. None of his mostly white colleagues showed signs of concern. Perhaps he'd misheard, he thought to himself. Later, he ran into another black colleague and started to ask, "During the opening session, did you hear—?" His colleague cut him off and said wryly, "Oh yeah, I heard it. Our district has a problem, and it's black students."

The district did have a problem. And to their credit, district leaders were committed to address it rather than brush over it. The problem wasn't the students, however; it was the district. District teachers and administrators hadn't yet become successful at serving their black students equally well. Perhaps it was lack of district support for professional development. Perhaps it was poor supervision from administrators or teachers with low expectations. Without more information, it's not certain. One thing, however, is certain. The framing of the problem determines what is investigated and shapes how we view and solve problems in our schools. If the problem is the students, adults are off the hook.

We've seen similar framing at many schools. We heard a middle school principal say, "Our problem is that we've been getting more and more English language learners." When we visited classrooms at this school, we found that teacher practice reflected this framing. Spanish speakers sat silently at the back of the classroom waiting until the teacher finished with the rest of the class before the teacher walked to the back to attempt to explain the assignment with the help of an online translator. The teaching remained exactly the same with the addition of translation for the Spanish speakers after English speakers had been taken care of. There were no additional visuals, no previewing of vocabulary, no real-world props or sentence stems to support language learners. What would teacher and administrator mindsets have been if the framing had been: "Our problem is that we haven't learned strategies for effectively teaching our newly arrived English language learners." Where are we locating the deficiency?

In their book, *How the Way We Talk Can Change the Way We Work*, authors Robert Kegan and Lisa Lahey point out the power of language to influence mindset. They describe opposing categories of language: complaint versus commitment; blame versus responsibility (see Table 9.1). In their words, "The language of complaint usually tells us, and others, what it is we can't stand. The language of commitment tells us (and possibly others) what it is we stand for."[4]

The way we as educators use language influences the way we perceive the ability of students of color. Language also shapes the way we view our role. The "achievement gap" conjures up a large chasm, like the Grand Canyon, with white students on one side and students of color across a seemingly insurmountable gulf. The "school-to-prison pipeline" evokes images of kindergarten

TABLE 9-1   Moving from complaint and blame to commitment and responsibility

Moving from the *"Language of Complaint"* to the *"Language of Commitment"*	
Language of Complaint	**Language of Commitment**
Explicitly expresses what we *cannot* do	Explicitly expresses what we stand for
Leaves us feeling like a whiny or cynical person	Leaves us feeling like a person filled with conviction and hope
Generates frustration	Generates vitalizing energy
Nontransformational—rarely goes anywhere beyond letting off steam	Transformational—anchors purpose-driven work

Moving from the *"Language of Blame"* to the *"Language of Personal Responsibility"*	
Language of Blame	**Language of Personal Responsibility**
Holds other people responsible for gaps between intentions and reality	Generates productive conversations that lead to problem-solving
Generates frustration and alienation in the speaker	Draws on the momentum of our commitments
Generates defensiveness in others	Raises questions for oneself
Nontransformational—deflects our attention to places where we have little or no influence	Transformational—directs our attention to places where we have maximum influence

Source: Robert Kegan and Lisa Lahey, *How the Way We Talk Can Change the Way We Work* (San Francisco: Jossey-Bass, 2001), pp. 30, 45. Modifications from The National Equity Project, Oakland, CA, www.nationalequityproject.org. Used with permission.

students of color hopping on a conveyor belt from the classroom to a life behind bars. These phrases not only reinforce biases but also remove a key actor, educators. How does our language shape the way we see our role in creating the gap or fueling the pipeline? How do we come to understand the role of unconscious bias in these phenomena? Recent studies document that the difference in average achievement between students of color and white students grows from kindergarten through high school.[5] How are we simultaneously investigating the effects of unconscious racial bias as a major contributor to the gap and the pipeline?

Consider the difference between these sentences, which are frequently used in schools:

a. Kids of color have higher failure rates than white students.
b. We are more effective at teaching our white students than our students of color.

Or these two:

a. Most kids of color are not on grade level in reading.
b. Either our reading curriculum or our implementation of the curriculum is not effective at helping our kids of color achieve grade level in reading.

Some might argue we're just parsing words, and they all mean the same thing in the end. However, the reason language is important is because it shapes the way we think about and locate a problem. That in turn determines where we dig for root causes.

We want to be clear that this isn't about blaming teachers. When teaching practices aren't producing equitable results, that problem is schoolwide and systemwide. Administrators cannot stand on the sidelines pointing fingers. The statement that "we aren't as effective teaching our black students as we are teaching our white students" implicates the entire system. How are the structures and systems set up for teachers to do successful work? Do teachers have the resources they need? Do administrators have a strategy for supporting teacher learning so that teachers are able to improve their practice? If teaching practice isn't effective, administrators have a responsibility to provide the right balance of support and accountability for teachers to improve it.

We've all probably heard people protest statements like the B sentences above. "But wait a minute," they might say. "Kids need to take responsibility for their own learning. We shouldn't be spoon-feeding them. That's not the teacher's responsibility." We agree that students have agency in their learning and need to take responsibility in school. Research increasingly shows that persistence and initiative are critical noncognitive skills and, importantly, that they need to be taught in school. We start from the premise that the purpose of schools is to teach. In the same way, the purpose of hospitals is to heal, the purpose of an auto repair shop is to fix cars, the purpose of trains is to transport people from one location to another. When schools aren't producing the outcome they are designed to produce, they have to take responsibility.

At the same time, some people say that schools are being blamed for problems much larger than the education sector. A disproportionately high percentage of students of color live in poverty, and poverty is something that can't be alleviated through education alone. An extremely thoughtful young teacher at Sarah's school agreed with this perspective—with a twist. She went to a lecture about education in Finland and learned all the ways its society addresses and proactively prevents poverty. She came into Sarah's office deeply troubled by the injustices in our society. She knew that many of her students of color lived below the poverty line and were deprived of adequate health care, food, and social services and were exposed to greater levels of toxins, racial profiling, and bias. "It's not fair to blame teachers when so many parts of our society are neglecting my students!" she cried. She said she wasn't going to let this go. She was going to raise awareness of the ways in which communities need to address poverty—disproportionately affecting children of color—and not blame schools.

Then this teacher recommitted to doing everything in her power to ensure her students succeeded in her class. Instead of absolving herself of responsibility, she continued to see her success as defined by how much she could help her children learn. She continued to monitor her success by looking at evidence of student learning. Like this teacher, inspiring leaders hold themselves and their schools accountable for ensuring all students learn. They understand their role in the problem as well as their responsibility and agency for solving it.

CHAPTER 10

Go Slow to Go Far

As a school leader, addressing unconscious racial bias requires constant grappling with a paradox. The work is urgent, yet requires patience. It must be done immediately, and to do it well requires time. If we push too hard, people may shut down and impede progress. However, every day that we aren't addressing our biases, they are holding back students of color. As leaders, we constantly find ourselves asking if we're effectively managing the tension in this paradox. As one leader said, when thinking about how much to push faculty, we need to constantly ask ourselves, "Who does this benefit and who does this hurt?"

We feel a sense of urgency because the status quo is harmful to our students. Doing nothing allows unconscious biases to continue to play out in schools. Unchecked, they diminish the learning of students of color and reinforce the unconscious racial biases of white students. A colleague told us that instead of thinking of her black and brown students as *underserved*, she considers them to be *overly harmed* by low expectations, increased suspicion, and complacency with poor instruction. Even in schools with gifted and skillful educators, our impact is diminished if we're not monitoring our bias. In other words, excellent teaching is necessary but not sufficient to ensure the success of black and brown students. Our students urgently need us to do better.

At the same time, the work requires patience because it's an adaptive challenge. Leadership experts Ronald Heifetz and Martin Linsky differentiate between technical challenges, which require learning new skill sets, and adaptive challenges, which require new mindsets.[1] Our work as leaders is to help people see that biases are not a distant abstraction but rather an up-close personal reality. Once people come to understand and believe that they are not immune, they're more willing to do the work of regularly monitoring their impact rather than trusting their intentions. This process is easier said than done. Helping people accept that they have blind spots requires a patient approach.

The leadership advice that we need to "go slow in order to go far" provides useful guidance. We're preparing for a marathon, not a sprint. As Capital City Head of School Karen Dresden says, "This isn't work that finishes; this is work that we're going to keep doing." As leaders, we've got to build the skills and stamina to engage in ongoing work over the long term.

TAKING A DEVELOPMENTAL APPROACH

It doesn't help to march into a school with our passions and conviction and not pay attention to our staff as individual learners. Bombarding them with the article or video or statistic that we found most profound isn't necessarily going to provide transformational learning for them. And transformational learning is the goal. At its heart, what this work requires is a belief that all adults can learn. However, like any meaningful learning process, learning about racial bias and its impact on us and our schools occurs in stages. It takes considerable effort over time, and at any given school, there will be a range of understanding across the staff.

We're the first to say that a developmental approach can feel frustrating. Parents have entrusted their precious children to our care. Do we tell them to hang on, that we'll get it right in a few years? This doesn't feel acceptable.

The question is, what is the most effective way to generate improvement? It's easy to make grand pronouncements about equity and excellence, uncompromising commitment, and the fact that inequities are unacceptable. We don't disagree with these statements; we've made them ourselves. However, anyone who has engaged in improvement work knows we can't simply mandate a change in beliefs. As artist and activist Patrisse Cullors said, "We can't policy our way out of racism."[2] We need a practical approach that yields practical results. That means starting with who the adult learners are and patiently building knowledge, skills, and courage. Skillful leaders create the conditions for transformational learning to occur.

This developmental process will look different for different schools. For example, over the last four years, one suburban, mostly white, public elementary school has transformed. The school now has the highest number of teachers of color in its district; the teachers have written and rolled out a schoolwide curriculum addressing racism and have been invited to present at Harvard about their work changing the school's culture from one that didn't discuss race to one that now teaches about racism in every grade, starting in kindergarten. Several staff members said that a key factor in their school's equity work is that the principal maintains a sense of urgency about the work. As one staff member said, "She is always pushing us to the next step."

Interestingly, this principal started the work at her school in a way that might seem slow to others. The staff began by reading two books—*Difficult Conversations*, which explains how to communicate directly even when emotions are high or when differences seem insurmountable, and *Mindset*, which helps people view mistakes and challenges as necessary steps to becoming smarter.[3] Neither book talks about race or racism. The books provide tools for people to talk to each other about difficult topics, cultivate mindsets that encourage people to embrace and not fear mistakes, and value critical feedback as crucial for learning. Together, they established a powerful foundation for how the staff would approach a challenging topic. This principal knew exactly where she was going.

The following year, the staff read books about racial identity. They chose to read one or more of a set of books by authors of different races exploring and describing their own racial identity. They discussed these in same-race groups and then together. The discussions provided opportunities to practice talking about race with colleagues in a mixed-race setting. The following year, the staff learned about racial bias and how it affected their teaching. At the same time, they selected a set of concepts (such as racism, prejudice, privilege, equity) that they all committed to teaching their students. During that year, a volunteer committee of teachers designed an anti-racism curriculum for teachers to use in every grade.

In the fourth year of development, the majority, but not every teacher, is comfortable teaching the basic concepts in the curriculum. Teaching partners from the design team support colleagues who are less confident with the material. Meanwhile, a growing group of staff members raise the need to investigate aspects of their practice for biases, and members of all races say they have come to understand themselves and their racial identity in new ways since working with this principal. Are all staff equally enthusiastic about these changes and the new curriculum? No. But a large group of teachers are, and that's enough to push the work forward.

Each school will have a different trajectory. For leaders, the key point is to remember that they're engaging faculty in a learning process. Lecturing people or directing them to do something they don't know how to do rarely leads to improvement.

Anticipate the Emotional Aspect of the Work

It's easy to forget in all our planning that working on unconscious racial bias is emotionally draining. We're not talking about abstract notions of educational theory. We're examining deep-rooted and often unexamined personal beliefs and actions we may not be proud to face. Leaders should expect people of all races to have strong emotional responses. An administrator at Capital City remembers a new black staff member having a strong reaction after the first small-group racial equity meeting. She came into the principal's office, closed the door and the blinds, and just cried. She said she'd never had open conversations about race with white people before, and she realized that she held stereotypes about her white colleagues that she would have to give up.

As leaders, we need to anticipate the emotional aspect of the work and ensure that we're creating an environment where people can face their discomfort, without running away. It helps when they know there's someone to talk to without judgment. When he was principal and his school started talking about race and racism, Tracey made sure there was a designated safe person whom staff members could talk to. He provided additional training for the school counselor to be that safe person. Her job was to help individual staff members work through their feelings and reactions in between whole-staff discussions of racism. Everyone knew that anything they said to her was confidential. Instead of complaining to colleagues in the teachers' lounge, they could talk to the counselor. So many people asked to meet with the school counselor after school and during the school day that Tracey removed all her extra duties and allowed her to shift her hours so she could regularly stay after school to help people.

Address Resistance

Leaders of change always face pushback. How they interpret and respond to that resistance makes a difference. We speak from experience when we caution leaders to beware of the binary mindset that sorts staff into opposing camps: bad/racist resister and good/nonracist nonresisters. When we simply dismiss some people as bad racists, we abandon our responsibility to help them grow. A developmental approach requires that we hear pushback with genuine curiosity to understand learners' perspectives and then use that information to plan the next steps. As Tracey likes to remind people, from a developmental perspective, there are no resisters, only learners. Some learners are at a very early stage in their understanding of how racism and unconscious racial bias operate in society and themselves.

This wasn't Sarah's approach when she entered the principal role. One year, concerned about the number of black boys being sent to the office, Sarah shared a reading with her staff, an excerpt from an essay critiquing white progressive teachers who do not recognize their biases in their work with children of color. She then had the teachers divide into groups to discuss the article.

Things immediately went downhill in the group Sarah joined. Diane, a veteran teacher, spoke first and dismissed the article out of hand. "I'm colorblind," this white woman explained firmly. "I treat all students the same, no matter what their race. This article doesn't make any sense to me." After this teacher's declaration, there was silence. Several young white teachers who had looked extremely uncomfortable from the beginning continued to sit across the table in silence. A black teacher asked the first teacher what colorblind meant to her, and Diane responded by continuing to insist that not paying any attention to race was the goal.

Sarah debated what to say. "You're wrong" was tempting but clearly not helpful. Sitting there silently didn't feel responsible. As a white person, it felt wrong to leave these comments unchallenged. So, she launched into an explanation of the false notion of colorblindness and then explained that because white people had internalized racism, they couldn't help but be racist. They had to face that fact in order to counter racism in society. Not surprisingly, this academic explanation did not lead to a collective amen from the group.

The meeting ended shortly after, and Diane got up from the table with a look that said, "This principal is crazier than I thought, and I can't wait to get out of here and back to my classroom." The teachers across the table looked even more uncomfortable and left quickly.

The unsolved question remained: how would Diane—as well as her silent colleagues—learn to recognize the influence of unconscious racial bias in their interactions with students? Just a few months earlier, this teacher had made casual comments to a black student that his family didn't care about his progress in school. Now this child was saying he didn't want to come to school anymore. Diane needed this work. Her students urgently needed her to learn from this work.

Using a developmental approach would have helped Sarah be a more effective leader in the discussion. If the focus were truly on learning, she would not have sought to suppress Diane's opinion. She would have sought to bring more voices into the conversation and to understand Diane's views more clearly. A discussion protocol would have ensured that all voices were heard as well.

Most importantly, a leader using a developmental approach would also use the information from this teacher's response—and the other teachers' anxiety—to better diagnose the learning the staff needed to do together. Probably none of these teachers had ever thought consciously about being white. Before thinking about cultural proficiency and the ideas in the article, these teachers needed to recognize how being white shaped their experience and view of the world. It would be hard to make progress without this step.

In Sarah's school, she was fortunate to have staff members who knew that a short reading at a staff meeting wasn't enough. These teacher leaders felt Sarah had misdiagnosed what the staff was ready for. While a fair number of the teachers were comfortable talking about race, a more strategic, long-term plan was needed. The school needed an ongoing, teacher-led focus on race and racial inequities in achievement.

Sarah and the teacher leaders established a task force of teachers who engaged in talking about race and learning about racial bias themselves and then led staff meetings in similar discussions focused on race and improving the school's work with African American students. When leading their first whole-staff meeting, the task force stood together in front of the library and explained, "We read this article in our task force and we learned a lot from it. At first, we disagreed about how the article applied to our staff. After talking about it and hearing different perspectives, we realized it was important to share with everyone. We want to hear how you think it applies to our staff." Not surprisingly, the results of this conversation were better. A few task force members reported that they continued informal conversations with colleagues on their teams in the days after that first meeting. The following year, multiple staff meetings focused explicitly on racial identity development.

In this example, staff resistance may have been due to too much, too soon, or simply a clumsy approach to engaging staff in self-examination. However, at other times, staff pushback may not have anything to do with the quality of the leader's approach. Instead, pushback occurs when white educators with the best intentions hear many of their fundamental assumptions questioned. They realize for the first time that they do have a racialized experience, and their blindness to the racial experiences of people of color in effect has distorted their view of reality. They see evidence that their personal unconscious beliefs and actions perpetuate inequality.

For white people coming to understand their whiteness for the first time, development along the learning continuum can be slow. Whiteness scholar Robin DiAngelo talks about her experience working with thousands of white people to help them understand whiteness.[4] Over time, she's come to recognize predictable patterns of how people respond. She's not surprised anymore. To the extent we can step back, depersonalize the resistance, and realize it's a predictable part of racial identity development, the better we'll be able to navigate it.

Some of the resistance we'll face comes from within. For leaders of all races, the desire to resolve feelings of disequilibrium and return to equanimity can lead us astray. We're always going to prefer being more comfortable. For example, we may feel inclined to put off the staff meeting talking about racial identity or we may feel it's too complicated to change the school climate survey to ask questions about race. When we anticipate the ways our own resistance may show up, we're better prepared to face it.

MAINTAINING A GROWTH MINDSET

Principals we spoke to who are doing this work had one consistent message to share: don't give up. Persist, even when things don't go well. Since the work is hard and new to most of us, we should expect to try something ten times and fail nine of those times. That tenth time is worth celebrating. Too often, the fear of messing up holds us back. The two of us continue to remind ourselves to have a growth mindset when we lead conversations about race and racism. Rather than fear mistakes, we view them as handholds that will pull us upward and forward. Yes, they're sometimes uncomfortable and messy. They're also valuable sources of learning.

One mistake is feeling that we have arrived. Most of us (of all races) want to feel we have eliminated our unconscious racial bias. We understand the impulse; after all, it's hard to regularly question our judgment. Especially after carefully examining ourselves, engaging in honest reflection, and facing some hard truths, we're tempted to feel confident that we've mastered the demon. Surely, we think, after all this work, our instincts will now line up with our aspirations. Be alert to being lured into complacency. Remember the toothbrushing metaphor? New gunk builds up each day; we need to stay alert.

Another helpful metaphor involves a rubber band. Longtime education reformer Richard Elmore alerts educators to how hard it is to make change within a system set up to produce a certain outcome. Most of the systems in the United States have long been designed to privilege white people and limit access, opportunity, and security for people of color. Changing such long-held beliefs and the systems that perpetuate them requires constant attention and vigilance, similar to stretching a rubber band. Elmore warns us that the moment we stop acting deliberately to make the change, things snap back into their original state.

Many times, Sarah has made progress in her understanding of the ways that bias operates within her thinking. She begins to recognize the larger system influencing her thinking and can reflect on situations and notice times when her responses are influenced by bias. She can see times when her treatment of white students or colleagues is different from her treatment of students or colleagues of color. Since she's glimpsed how the system operates, she thinks she can be free of its influence. Vigilance loosens. She stops questioning her impact, stops being alert to the pernicious ways bias seeps in. Most dangerously, she loses that humble mindset necessary for growth, and defensiveness returns. Without diligence, the rubber band returns to its original shape.

She returns to this easier, more comfortable state until caught up short by a trusted colleague like Tracey reflecting the ways unconscious bias may be manifesting in actions: "Did you consider other ways students might have experienced that behavior? That policy? Are you relying too much on your intentions here?"

Rather than reassuring ourselves that we're not biased, we can instead cultivate *ongoing racial humility*. We may think we see everything, but we're still wearing blinders. This is where a growth mindset is invaluable. We want to continually question our views and assessments to expand our worldview.

Another pitfall is the perpetual temptation to make the work easier. Once we begin collectively examining the impact of our biases and have some difficult conversations and perhaps some subsequent breakthroughs, we may feel that everything will be easier henceforth. It's a remarkable accomplishment to create an environment where people can talk to each other about racism and bias. After the long road to get there, we may avoid introducing disagreement or anything that would produce discomfort out of fear of ruining the new environment we've created. However, if progress comes from engaging in uncomfortable conversations, we can't stop having them. Leaders who hold a growth mindset know to embrace, not avoid, that which challenges us the most.

Over time, as staff members become increasingly comfortable speaking their truth, more difficult conversations will surface. This is good, even though it may not feel that way. Pursuing disagreements, misunderstandings, and courageous conversations strengthens our brave community and helps us make progress.

Making mistakes will be easier when we see ourselves as learners. It doesn't help to beat up ourselves or others for not being where we want to be. We can't skip stages. Learners don't leapfrog from addition to calculus. In a developmental process, the only way to the goal is through the hard work of learning. We're inspired by the slogan of one school we've worked with: "jump in, get stuck, push through."[5]

Affirm and Expect Progress

Tracey once asked a group of principals, "What is the most prevalent feeling that comes to you when you think about going to a session on race and racism? It could be positive or negative, just whatever comes up for you." Every emotion these principals named was negative. This was a particularly pressing problem for Tracey because he was about to lead these administrators into a campus workshop on race and racism. He worried that their negative mindset would inhibit their learning. It's hard to be open-minded when you're already sure the situation will be awful.

Tracey then asked, "What if this were the best experience ever? How would you feel?" He knew he couldn't tell people to change their expectations. However, he could encourage people to be aware of their emotions and how they might affect their experience. The principals shared afterward that while the experience wasn't transforming for them—their response didn't match their emotions for "best experience ever"—they were more aware of the ways their personal emotions were affecting their engagement with the material. When we expect something to be negative, we're more likely to enter that conversation on the defensive, to withhold our real questions and feelings, and to resist anything unfamiliar. Remembering that people come loaded with all sorts of baggage can help us frame the conversation for more productive engagement.

After a conversation about racial bias with mostly white colleagues, a black principal named Alicia said that she wished conversations about race and racism didn't always have to feel so bad. "Couldn't we have a conversation that felt good?" she asked. Progress along these lines might change the reaction of principals like those Tracey surveyed. The point isn't to take away the discomfort that leads to learning. We don't think Alicia was asking for it to feel easy. A really challenging workout at the gym or hard but honest conversation with a spouse or child can feel extremely difficult, yet at the end, the experience feels worthwhile, like you ended in a stronger place than where you started. Couldn't our work together confronting and addressing the impact of our biases feel like that? What if we approached this work with an expectation of growing, of making progress?

Alicia may also have been referring to the unequal division of labor in this work. Too often, white people don't carry their fair share. We see this in moments when white people go silent, withdraw from the conversation, and look around warily. People of color like Alicia are left to decide whether or not to take up the work of moving the conversation forward and risk potentially being seen as insensitive, aggressive, or accusatory. This is a heavy burden. Couldn't the leaders of that conversation do something to lift that burden from Alicia's shoulders and help others carry it? Thoughtful framing can help more people, especially white people, leave their comfort zones to engage.

Do we introduce the work in heavy, ponderous tones, with a grim look, like we're all about to get a good scolding? Or do we applaud our staff for engaging in proactive, constructive work that builds a strong community with better outcome for our students? Do we pause to recognize how much we're learning about each other and how valuable this is for our collaboration? Do we celebrate that this is a staff that seeks to make our intentions reality, a staff that loves students, and that's why we're focusing on our impact? When our framing sounds more like a dirge, it's no wonder people act as if they're at a funeral. Instead of dreading the discomfort, let's try to run toward it the way our best students relish challenging assignments. We're building something together; it's going to require lots of hard work, and we can't wait to reap the fruits of our labors.

Take Care of Ourselves

The airlines regularly remind us that we need to put on our own oxygen mask first before helping others. The same advice holds true in schools. To advance this work, leaders need to take care of themselves. As with many aspects of being a school leader, this can be challenging.

Like most leaders we know, we rely on same-race colleagues, family, and friends to be the equivalent of our oxygen mask. It helps to talk to someone who intuitively understands our racial perspective. It also helps when these trusted partners understand the work, will sympathize with how hard it is, and will encourage us to stick with it when the going gets tough.

Leaders of color need other, like-minded leaders of color to debrief with. It can be hard to continue to be patient, to hold a space of compassion for white staff members who benefit so much from the system that is simultaneously oppressive to the person of color leading the effort. Leaders of color have a difficult choice. Leading this work will be emotionally taxing. This emotional strain—likely unnoticed by most white staff—comes on top of an already stressful job. Is it too much? Can white staff take the lead instead? One self-care strategy is to ensure white people are putting their shoulder to this plow.

White leaders need colleagues who will have compassion for the challenge but won't seek to reduce the disequilibrium. Because experiencing that disorientation is often the richest source of learning, these colleagues need to be careful not to try to make it better. White people need a colleague who won't coddle but rather will help them feel ready to return to the work.

As leaders, we also need to look out for the teachers who are leading this effort and remember how draining it is for them. Inevitably, at any given school, some people carry more than their share. In most schools, people of color carry the bulk of the burden. As leaders, we need to be careful not to expect the staff of color to carry this work. This is worth repeating because even if, as leaders ourselves, we are mindful of not expecting staff of color to carry the lion's share, white faculty members may instinctively look to faculty of color for guidance, consolation, or validation that they are good white people. This unofficial work is often invisible, goes unrecognized, and tends to be immensely draining for faculty of color. Leaders can alert all staff to this pattern in order to change the dynamic.

Recognize Our Agency

Addressing the effects of racism can feel futile at times. Like battling the massive manufacturing industry that produces the smog we breathe, trying to address racism is a massive task. We're up against the influence of the all-powerful media, hundreds of years of conditioning, deeply embedded instincts, and our strongly held sense of identity. Some school leaders will feel woefully inexperienced, others too tired, others afraid for their jobs. The work is daunting, and many before us have said that it's too big to tackle, too messy to risk, or too far beyond their skill set.

Yet every day individual children of color show up to our schools. They learn lessons that either accelerate or diminish their learning. As school leaders we are in a position to make a difference. Together, with teacher leaders, we develop our school's goals and agenda, we make decisions about how time is allocated, we point the spotlight on what needs attention, and we shape the practice of our staff. Above all, school leaders set the vision for schools. We describe the end goal—the kind of community our school strives to be each day.

Capital City principal Laina Cox reminds us to tackle racial equity work the same way we would tackle bringing STEM or a reading initiative or any other improvement effort into the building. Start small. Be strategic. In her charismatic way, Cox passionately implores her colleagues:

Start small. If you can't give an hour a month to it, figure out what you can give to it and just commit to it. The key is just to start! Pilot it with folks who want to. Survey your staff and get a pulse of who wants to attempt it. Even if it's just two people, attempt it. If you can't find any time at all, find a text that you're going to give your staff. Find a book that you can pull quotes from and put in your bulletin each week. Host voluntary lunch chats each week. No one is saying you have to go from zero to a hundred. Just do something![6]

There are no easy fixes. What's been present for hundreds of years will not disappear after one staff meeting, or even after a year of staff meetings. However, Cox is right. Leaders have to take action. When we remain paralyzed, all of our students suffer, and students of color are denied their full potential. We won't make any progress if we don't try to make *some* progress. As philosopher Lao Tzu said, "A journey of a thousand miles begins with a single step." School leaders have agency in this work. Let's start the journey.

Supporting Resources

There is no way we can include a comprehensive list of resources for leaders to use with their staff. There are too many great books, videos, and articles to name. However, we've selected a few items because they might be of practical use to school leaders and their staffs. Many are short and focused enough for the purposes of viewing or reading during a staff or team meeting. Some are scholarly and provide more background information.

CHAPTER 1: DO WE HAVE A BIAS PROBLEM?

- *State of the Science: Implicit Bias Review.* Annual report from The Kirwan Institute for the Study of Race and Ethnicity at The Ohio State University describing the latest research on implicit bias in different sectors from health and housing to education and criminal justice.
- *Race: The Power of an Illusion*, by California Newsreel. Compelling documentary in three parts debunking myths about race and describing the ways government policies created racial inequities.
- *What's Race Got to Do With It?: How Current School Reform Policy Maintains Racial and Economic Inequality*, edited by Bree Picower and Edwin Mayorga (Peter Lang, Inc., 2015). This book explores the influence of entrenched racism through the system of education in the United States.
- "The Problem We All Live With," by Nikole Hannah-Jones. Audio show on *This American Life* that describes how racism manifests in school districts today. Hannah-Jones examines the school district that Michael Brown attended in Missouri.

- *The Color of Law: A Forgotten History of How Our Government Segregated America*, by Richard Rothstein (Liveright, 2018). Economist Rothstein demonstrates how explicit government policies produced racially segregated communities, which lead to racial inequalities in a variety of sectors. The author has also written short articles about the same topic. One is: "From Ferguson to Baltimore: The Fruits of Government-Sponsored Segregation," https://www.epi.org/blog/from-ferguson-to-baltimore-the-fruits-of-government-sponsored-segregation/.

CHAPTER 2: START WITH OURSELVES

- *Immunity to Change: How to Overcome It and Unlock the Potential in Yourself and Your Organization*, by Robert Kegan and Lisa Lahey (Harvard Business Review Press, 2009). This book provides a useful framework to help leaders overcome self-imposed and significant internal barriers, fears, and anxieties.
- *Why Are All the Black Kids Sitting Together in the Cafeteria?: And Other Conversations About Race*, by Beverly Daniel Tatum (Basic Books, 2017). This book explores the psychology of racism and racial identity development. Chapter 1 can be used as a stand-alone, succinct, and accessible explanation of racism and its contemporary manifestation. Subsequent chapters describe the characteristics of racial identity development for different racial groups.
- *Leadership and Self-Deception: Getting Out of the Box*, by The Arbinger Institute (Berrett-Koehler Publishers, 2018). This book helps leaders consider how the way they frame problems and participate in negative "self-talk" can inhibit positive relationships with others.
- *Waking Up White*, and Finding Myself in the Story of Race, by Debby Irving (Elephant Room Press, 2014). A white woman tells her own story of racial identity development including many honest reflections on how she came to grips with her own racial biases.
- *Between the World and Me*, by Ta-Nehisi Coates (Spiegel & Grau, 2015). This *New York Times* bestseller documents the author's personal story of understanding what it means to be black in America in the format of a letter to his adolescent son.

CHAPTER 3: NORMALIZE TALKING ABOUT RACE AND BIAS

- *So You Want to Talk About Race*, by Ijeoma Oluo (Seal Press, 2018). A collection of short chapters on common questions white people ask about race.
- Twenty-five mini-films for exploring race, bias, and identity with students. A *New York Times*–curated list of short (generally under ten minutes) films that show people of different races talking about their racial identity and experience. The suggested questions for use with the videos are for students but could also be used with adults.
- "How to overcome our biases? Walk boldly toward them," TED talk, by Verna Myers. Myers explains unconscious bias and exhorts listeners to address it directly. She provides practical strategies for doing so.
- "Who Me, Biased?," *New York Times* series on implicit bias. These six videos of three to four minutes each explain current research on unconscious racial bias.
- TEDx talk: "How I Learned to Stop Worrying and Love Discussing Race," by Jay Smooth, https://www.youtube.com/watch?v=MbdxeFcQtaU. In this accessible and humorous TEDx talk, Smooth explains common pitfalls and fears in talking about race and offers suggestions for how to normalize these conversations.
- Harvard Project Implicit: https://implicit.harvard.edu/implicit/takeatest. html. An interactive site where anyone can take a variety of short, online tests that assess unconscious biases. Participants can view their results and how they compare to other test takers.
- *The Person You Mean to Be: How Good People Fight Bias*, by Dolly Chugh (Harper Business, 2018). A business school professor provides the research basis for and explains how we are all influenced by a variety of unconscious biases that prevent us from fulfilling our intentions.

CHAPTER 4: CULTIVATE A BRAVE COMMUNITY

- *Courageous Conversations About Race: A Field Guide for Achieving Equity in Schools*, by Glenn Singleton (Corwin, 2014). A practical guide for starting conversations about race with educator colleagues. Each chapter can be read alone and includes suggested discussion questions and activities.

- *Everyday Antiracism: Getting Real About Race in School*, edited by Mica Pollock (The New Press, 2008). A collection of short articles by leading authors on race and racism who describe practical steps teachers can take to increase racial equity and address racism in their classrooms and schools.

CHAPTER 5: WHOSE COMFORT ARE WE PRIORITIZING?

- *White Fragility: Why It's So Hard for White People to Talk About Racism*, by Robin DiAngelo (Beacon Press, 2018). This white author addresses the common reactions white people have when facing their own racism and how these reactions reinforce the racism they say they oppose.
- "White privilege: unpacking the invisible knapsack," by Peggy McIntosh, https://nationalseedproject.org/Key-SEED-Texts/white-privilege-unpacking-the-invisible-knapsack. In this classic article, McIntosh describes the ways she benefits from the privileges of being white in a racist society.
- *Good White People: The Problem with Middle-Class White Anti-Racism*, by Shannon Sullivan (SUNY Press, 2014). This book explores the nuances of white-middle-class racism and exposes the myths of self-proclaimed white nonracists.

CHAPTER 6: INVESTIGATING THE RACIAL CLIMATE IN OUR SCHOOLS

- *Subtractive Schooling: U.S.-Mexican Youth and the Politics of Caring*, by Angela Valenzuela (State University of New York Press, 1999). This book is an ethnography of the experiences of a variety of Latino/a students in a high school in Texas. Valenzuela explains the ways in which school climate can negatively affect students of color.
- Documentary: *What's Race Got to Do With It?*, by California Newsreel. This film documents a racially diverse group of college students as they meet over time to discuss their racial identities and experiences of racism on campus.

CHAPTER 7: EXAMINING INSTRUCTION AND CLASSROOM CLIMATE

- *For White Folks Who Teach in the Hood . . . and the Rest of Y'all Too: Reality Pedagogy and Urban Education*, by Christopher Emdin (Beacon Press, 2017). Describes teaching practices that are culturally responsive and respectful of students of color.
- *Pygmalion in the Classroom: Teacher Expectation and Pupils' Intellectual Development*, by Robert Rosenthal and Lenore Jacobson (Crown House Publishing, 2003). This study explores the impact of teacher expectations on students' academic outcomes.
- Dr. Pedro Noguera on Reframing the "Color of Discipline," by The Equity Alliance. In this brief interview, Dr. Noguera responds to common questions about racially disparate discipline practices, explains how unconscious bias plays a role, and offers suggestions to address these inequalities.
- AERA 2018 Presidential Address: Deborah Loewenberg Ball, https://www.youtube.com/watch?time_continue=4982&v=JGzQ7O_SIYY, May 4, 2018. In her speech (about an hour and twenty minutes into the talk), Dr. Deborah Ball describes "discretionary spaces" in teaching, how our biases inform our responses, and how these responses can reinforce or disrupt racism.
- *Pushout: The Criminalization of Black Girls in Schools*, by Monique Morris (The New Press, 2016). This book explains the racial biases that lead to black girls experiencing disproportionately harsh punishment in school and what educators can do to address this disparity.

CHAPTER 8: ADDRESSING UNCONSCIOUS BIAS IN ACADEMICS

- *Solving Disproportionality and Achieving Equity: A Leader's Guide to Using Data to Change Hearts and Minds*, by Edward A. Fergus (Corwin, 2017). This book explains how racial biases hold back students of color and provides a road map for how schools can collect and analyze data as well as how they can build cultural competency among staff.
- *Standards and Promising Practices for Schools Educating Boys of Color*, developed by Coalition of Schools Educating Boys of Color, www.coseboc.

org. Describes best school and classroom practices for supporting high achievement of boys of color.

- *Grading for Equity: What It Is, Why It Matters, and How It Can Transform Schools and Classrooms*, by Joe Feldman (Corwin, 2018). This book explains how traditional grading systems are susceptible to racial bias and too often are unchanged from a century ago when they were designed to deny opportunity to subgroups of students. The book includes practical suggestions for more equitable grading policies and practices.
- "Equal Opportunity for Deeper Learning" by Pedro Noguera, Linda Darling-Hammond, and Diane Friedlaender, www.jff.org/deeperlearning, 2015. This paper explains the importance of providing equitable access to high-quality instruction to all students, including students of color who have historically been denied such access.

CHAPTER 9: REFRAMING THE PROBLEM

- "Changing the Discourse in Schools," by Eugene Eubanks, Ralph Parish, and Dianne Smith, in *Race, Ethnicity, and Multiculturalism Policy and Practice* (Garland Publishing, Inc., 1994), chapter 5. This article explains how the language we unconsciously use in schools reinforces entrenched racial inequalities. The authors offer an alternative discourse to change outcomes in schools. Also available with a useful T-chart at https://ncs. uchicago.edu/sites/ncs.uchicago.edu/files/uploads/tools/NCS_PS_Toolkit_DPL_Set_B_ChangingTheDiscourse.pdf.
- *The Dreamkeepers: Successful Teachers of African American Children*, 2nd ed., by Gloria Ladson-Billings (Jossey-Bass, 2009). The author observed teachers who got excellent results from black students and captured the practices that led to those outcomes.
- *The Guide for White Women Who Teach Black Boys*, edited by Eddie Moore Jr., Ali Michael, and Marguerite W. Penick-Parks (Corwin, 2017). A collection of short essays by different authors with advice for white teachers to face their own biases, navigate being called racist, hear the perspective of a black student's mother, and other, often first-person stories.
- *Difficult Conversations: How to Discuss What Matters Most*, by Douglas Stone, Bruce Patton, and Sheila Heen (Penguin Books, 2010). This book

explains how people can engage in difficult conversations without defensiveness, with an increased capacity to listen, and an ability to improve relationships.

CHAPTER 10: GO SLOW TO GO FAR

- *Despite the Best Intentions: How Racial Inequality Thrives in Good Schools*, by Amanda Lewis and John Diamond (Oxford University Press, 2019). The authors spent years observing and documenting the ways racial biases play out in a school despite teachers' and administrators' explicit advocacy of racial equity and social justice.
- *In Over Our Heads: The Mental Demands of Modern Life*, by Robert Kegan (Harvard University Press, 1998). This book challenges readers to rethink our internal meaning-making systems and explores the role of adult development with relation to our capacity to broaden our worldview.
- "What's Missing from the Conversation: The Growth Mindset in Cultural Competency," by Rosetta Eun Ryong Lee, www.nais.org, 2015. In this article, the author recommends that educators embrace a growth mindset when embarking on collaborative, anti-racism work.

PARTICIPATE IN WORKSHOPS TO CONTINUE TO BUILD SKILLS TO LEAD ANTI-RACISM WORK AT YOUR SCHOOL

- The National SEED Project, founded by Peggy McIntosh, prepares educators to facilitate seminars at their schools that increase a school's capacity to address racism and other forms of oppression.
- The National Equity Project trains school leaders and coaches to address racial inequities in their schools.
- Beyond Diversity teaches educators about race and racism and how to return to their schools with strategies to address racial inequities.
- Interaction Institute for Social Change provides training for facilitators seeking to lead conversations about racial justice. It also has an active blog with perspectives on leading and facilitating for racial justice.
- Seek out other organizations in your community.

Notes

Introduction

1. Ronald A. Heifitz, Marty Linsky, and Alexander Grashow, *The Practice of Adaptive Leadership: Tools and Tactics for Changing Your Organization and the World* (Boston: Harvard Business School Press, 2009).
2. Eduardo Bonilla-Silva, *Racism Without Racists: Color-Blind Racism and the Persistence of Racial Inequality in the United States* (Lanham, MD: Rowman & Littlefield, 2003).
3. We have disclosed names only when discussing positive leaders; other identities have been masked.

Chapter 1

1. Amanda E. Lewis and John B. Diamond, *Despite the Best Intentions: How Racial Inequality Thrives in Good Schools* (New York: Oxford University Press, 2017).
2. Saleem Reshamwala, "Who Me, Biased?," *New York Times* Video, 2016, https://www.nytimes.com/video/who-me-biased; Rebecca Knight, "7 Practical Ways to Reduce Bias in Your Hiring Process," *Harvard Business Review*, June 12, 2017, https://hbr.org/2017/06/7-practical-ways-to-reduce-bias-in-your-hiring-process; Dennis Yang, "How Unconscious Bias Is Holding Your Company Back," *Fortune*, January 14, 2017, http://fortune.com/2017/01/14/unconscious-bias-leadership-career-advice-diversity/.
3. Reshamwala, "Who Me, Biased?"
4. Mahzarin R. Banaji and Anthony G. Greenwald, *Blindspot: Hidden Biases of Good People* (New York: Delacorte Press, 2013).
5. Rich Morin, "Exploring Racial Bias Among Biracial and Single-Race Adults: The IAT" (Washington, DC: Pew Research Center, 2015).
6. Beverly Daniel Tatum, *Why Are All the Black Kids Sitting Together in the Cafeteria?: And Other Conversations About Race* (New York: Basic Books, 1997), 5–6.
7. See the film *Race: The Power of An Illusion* for a demonstration of this experiment. California Newsreel, in association with the Independent Television Service, *Race: The Power of an Illusion* (San Francisco: California Newsreel, 2003).
8. Ian Holmes, "What Happens When Geneticists Talk Sloppily About Race," *The Atlantic*, April 25, 2018, https://www.theatlantic.com/science/archive/2018/04/reich-genetics-racism/558818/.

9. Richard Rothstein, *The Color of Law: A Forgotten History of How Our Government Segregated America* (New York: Liveright Publishing Corporation, 2017).

10. Nikole Hannah-Jones, interviewed by Nancy Updike, *This American Life*, NPR, November 22, 2013, https://www.thisamericanlife.org/512/house-rules.

11. Rothstein, *The Color of Law*, xii.

12. Rachel L. Swarns, "Biased Lending Evolves, and Blacks Face Trouble Getting Mortgages," *New York Times*, October 30, 2015, https://www.nytimes.com/2015/10/31/nyregion/hudson -city-bank-settlement.html?_r=0.

13. Brentin Mock, "Remember Redlining? It's Alive and Evolving," *The Atlantic*, October 8, 2015, https://www.theatlantic.com/politics/archive/2015/10/remember -redlining-its-alive-and-evolving/433065/.

14. Daniel Cox, Juhem Navarro-Rivera, and Robert P. Jones, *Race, Religion, and Political Affiliation of Americans' Core Social Networks* (Washington, DC: Public Religion Research Institute, 2016), https://www.prri.org/research/poll-race-religion-politics-americans -social-networks/.

15. This statistic varied only slightly in different regions of the country (82% for white people in the Midwest to 77% in the South) with the fewest people in complete racial isolation in the West with 68%.

16. Stacy L. Smith, Marc Choueiti, and Dr. Katherine Pieper, "Inequality in 800 Popular Films," USC Annenberg School for Communication and Journalism: Media, Diversity, and Social Change Initiative, 2016, https://annenberg.usc.edu/news/faculty-research /hollywood-equality-all-talk-little-action.

17. K. D. Kinzler and E. S. Spelke, "Do Infants Show Social Preferences for People Differing in Race?," *Cognition* 119, no. 1 (2011): 1–9, doi:10.1016/j.cognition.2010.10.019; A. B. Doyle and F. E. Aboud, "A Longitudinal Study of White Children's Racial Prejudice as a Social-Cognitive Development," *Merrill-Palmer Quarterly* 41, no. 2 (1995): 209–228.

18. P. Jordan and M. Hernandez-Reif, "Reexamination of Young Children's Racial Attitudes and Skin Tone Preferences," *Journal of Black Psychology* 35, no. 3 (2009): 388–403.

19. K. Clark and M. Clark, "Racial Identification and Preference in Negro Children," in *Readings in Social Psychology* (New York: Henry Holt and Company, 1947), 169–78.

20. Salvatore Colleluori and Daniel Angster, "New York City Television Stations Continue Disproportionate Coverage Of Black Crime," Media Matters, March 23, 2015, https://www .mediamatters.org/research/2015/03/23/report-new-york-city-television-stations-contin /202553.

21. Jessica Grosholz and Charis Kubrin, "Crime in the News: How Crimes, Offenders and Victims Are Portrayed in the Media," *Journal of Criminal Justice and Popular Culture* 14 (2007): 59–83.

22. A. R. Green, D. R. Carney, D. J. Pallin, L. H. Ngo, K. L. Raymond, L. I. Iezzoni, and M. R. Banaji, "Implicit Bias among Physicians and its Prediction of Thrombolysis Decisions for Black and White Patients," *Journal of General Internal Medicine* 22, no. 9 (2007): 1231–38, http://doi.org/10.1007/s11606-007-0258-5.

23. J. C. Livaudais, D. L. Hershman, L. Habel, L. Kushi, S. L. Gomez, C. I. Li, . . . G. D. Coronado, "Racial/ethnic Differences in Initiation of Adjuvant Hormonal Therapy among Women with Hormone Receptor-positive Breast Cancer," *Breast Cancer Research and Treatment* 131, no. 2 (2012): 607–617, http://doi.org/10.1007/s10549-011-1762-1; S. Trawalter, K. M. Hoffman, and A. Waytz "Racial Bias in Perceptions of Others' Pain," *PLoS ONE* 7, no. 11 (2012): e48546, https://doi.org/10.1371/journal.pone.0048546.

24. J. Correll, B. Park, C. M. Judd, and B. W. Wittenbrink, "The Police Officer's Dilemma: Using Ethnicity to Disambiguate Potentially Threatening Individuals," *Journal of Personality and Social Psychology* 83 (2002): 1314–29; A. G. Greenwald, M. A. Oakes, and H. Hoffman, "Targets of Discrimination: Effects of Race on Responses to Weapons Holders," *Journal of Experimental Social Psychology* 39 (2003): 399–405; B. K. Payne, "Prejudice and Perception: The Role of Automatic and Controlled Processes in Misperceiving a Weapon," *Journal of Personality and Social Psychology* 81 (2001): 1–12; B. K. Payne, A. J. Lambert, and L. L. Jacoby, "Best Laid Plans: Effects of Goals on Accessibility Bias and Cognitive Control in Race-Based Misperceptions of Weapons," *Journal of Experimental Social Psychology* 38 (2002): 384–96; B. K. Payne, "Weapon Bias Split-Second Decisions and Unintended Stereotyping," *Current Directions in Psychological Science* 15 (2006): 287–91.

25. Sam Scott, "A Hard Look at How We See Race," *Stanford Magazine*, September/October 2015, https://alumni.stanford.edu/get/page/magazine/article/?article_id=80755.

26. F. Baumgartner, L. Christiani, D. Epp, K. Roach, and K. Shoub, "Racial Disparities in Traffic Stop Outcomes," Duke Forum for Law and Social Change, 2017, retrieved from https://www.unc.edu/~fbaum/articles/BaumgartnerEtAl-2017-Duke Forum-RacialDisparitiesInTrafficStops.pdf.

27. A. Austin, *The Unfinished March: An Overview*, Economic Policy Institute Report, 2013, retrieved from http://www.epi.org/publication/unfinished-march-overview/.

28. K. Neckerman and J. Kirschenman, "Hiring Strategies, Racial Bias, and Inner-City Workers," *Social Problems* 38, no. 4 (1991): 433–47.

29. Marianne Bertrand and Sendhil Mullainathan, "Are Emily and Greg More Employable Than Lakisha and Jamal? A Field Experiment on Labor Market Discrimination," *American Economic Review* 94, no. 4 (2004): 991–1013, https://www.aeaweb.org/articles?id=10.1257/0002828042002561.

30. Katherine L. Milkman, Modupe Akinola, and Dolly Chugh, "What Happens Before? A Field Experiment Exploring How Pay and Representation Differentially Shape Bias on the Pathway into Organizations," *Journal of Applied Psychology* 100, no. 6 (2015): 1678.

31. Bertrand and Mullainathan, "Are Emily and Greg More Employable Than Lakisha and Jamal?"

32. D. J. Losen, "Discipline Policies, Successful Schools, and Racial Justice" (Boulder, CO: National Education Policy Center, 2011), retrieved from http://nepc.colorado.edu/publication/discipline-policies, August 12, 2018.

33. Jason A. Okonofua and Jennifer L. Eberhardt, "Two Strikes: Race and the Disciplining of Young Students," *Psychological Science* 26, no. 5 (2015): 617–24.

34. Robert Rosenthal and Lenore Jacobson, "Pygmalion in the Classroom," *The Urban Review* 3, no. 1 (1968): 16–20

35. Amanda E. Lewis and John B. Diamond, *Despite the Best Intentions: How Racial Inequality Thrives in Good Schools* (New York: Oxford University Press, 2017).

Chapter 2

1. Robin DiAngelo, *What Does it Mean to be White?: Developing White Racial Literacy* (New York: Peter Lang, 2016), 23–24.

2. Eddie Moore Jr., Ali Michael, and Marguerite W. Penick-Parks, *The Guide for White Women Who Teach Black Boys* (Thousand Oaks, CA: Corwin, 2018), 72.

3. Ta-Nehisi Coates, "Playing the Racist Card," *Slate*, March 14, 2008, http://www.slate.com/articles/news_and_politics/hey_wait_a_minute/2008/03/playing_the_racist_card.single.html.

4. Sarah E. Fiarman, "Unconscious Bias: When Good Intentions Aren't Enough," *Educational Leadership* 74, no. 3 (November 2016): 10–15.

5. Robert Kegan and Lisa Lahey, *How the Way We Talk Can Change the Way We Work* (San Francisco: Jossey-Bass, 2001).

6. Jay Smooth, "How I Learned to Stop Worrying and Love Discussing Race," TED talk, November 15, 2011, https://www.youtube.com/watch?v=MbdxeFcQtaU.

Chapter 3

1. Eddie Moore Jr., Ali Michael, and Marguerite W. Penick-Parks, *The Guide for White Women Who Teach Black Boys* (Thousand Oaks, CA: Corwin, 2018), 4.

2. Ibid., 4.

3. Verna Myers, "How to Overcome Our Biases? Walk Boldly Toward Them," TEDxBeaconStreet, November 2014, https://www.ted.com/talks/verna_myers_how_to_overcome_our_biases_walk_boldly_toward_them.

4. As cited in Shannon Sullivan, *Good White People: The Problem with Middle-Class White Anti-Racism* (Albany: State University of New York Press, 2014), 4.

5. Mica Pollock, *Colormute: Race Talk Dilemmas in an American School* (Princeton, NJ: Princeton University Press, 2004).

6. Sullivan, *Good White People: The Problem with Middle-Class White Anti-Racism.*

7. This section includes material from chapter 8 of Sarah Fiarman, *Becoming a School Principal* (Cambridge: Harvard Education Press, 2015), 168. Used with permission.

8. Elizabeth A. City and Danique A. Dolly, "Tending the Fire," *Educational Leadership* 74, no. 8 (2017): 38–41.

9. Beverly Daniel Tatum, *Why Are All the Black Kids Sitting Together in the Cafeteria?: And Other Conversations About Race* (New York: Basic Books, 1997).

10. Karen Dresden (Head of School, Capital City Public Charter School), in discussion with coauthor Sarah Fiarman, Friday, June 30, 2017.
11. Myra Brooks, presentation at "EL Education Atlantic Regional Leadership Cohort" (Charleston, SC, October 2016).
12. Glenn E. Singleton, *Courageous Conversations About Race: A Field Guide for Achieving Equity in Schools* (Thousand Oaks, CA: Corwin, 2015), 56–58.
13. Usable Knowledge, "Talking About Race in Mostly White Schools," https://www.gse .harvard.edu/news/uk/17/04/talking-about-race-mostly-white-schools?utm_source =facebook&utm_medium=social&utm_term=One+and+All%2CUsable+Knowledge &utm_content&utm_campaign=HGSE+Social.
14. Emily Style, "Curriculum as Encounter: Selves and Shelves," *English Journal* 103, no. 5 (2014): 67–74.
15. For these and other protocols, see National School Reform Faculty, "Protocols and Activities from A to Z," https://www.nsrfharmony.org/protocols/ or www.schoolreforminitiative .org
16. Teaching Tolerance, "Toolkit for Beyond the Knapsack," https://www.tolerance.org /magazine/spring-2014/toolkit-for-beyond-the-knapsack.
17. Dresden, in discussion with Fiarman.

Chapter 4

1. James Baldwin, "The Creative Process," *The Price of the Ticket: Collected Nonfiction* (New York: St. Martin's Press, 1985).
2. Jay Smooth, "How I Learned to Stop Worrying and Love Discussing Race," TED talk, November 15, 2011, https://www.youtube.com/watch?v=MbdxeFcQtaU.
3. Lisa Delpit, *Other People's Children: Cultural Conflict in the Classroom* (New York: The New Press, 1995).
4. Janine de Novais, "Brave Community: Teaching and Learning Race in College in the 21st Century" Harvard Graduate School of Education dissertation, 2017.
5. Robert Kegan and Lisa Lahey, *How the Way We Talk Can Change the Way We Work* (San Francisco: Jossey-Bass, 2001), 108–110.
6. Glenn E. Singleton, *Courageous Conversations About Race: A Field Guide for Achieving Equity in Schools* (Thousand Oaks, CA: Corwin, 2015), 70.
7. Karen Dresden (Head of School, Capital City Public Charter School), in discussion with coauthor Sarah Fiarman, Friday, June 30, 2017.
8. Beverly Daniel Tatum, "Cultivating the Trust of Black Parents," in *Everyday Anti-Racism*, Mica Pollock, ed. (New York: The New Press, 2008), 310–13.
9. Carol Dweck, *Mindset: The New Psychology of Success* (New York: Ballantine Books, 2008).
10. Robin J. DiAngelo, *What Does It Mean to Be White?: Developing White Racial Literacy* (New York: Peter Lang, 2012).

Chapter 5

1. Robin DiAngelo, *White Fragility: Why It's So Hard for White People to Talk About Racism* (Boston: Beacon Press, 2018).
2. Karen Dresden (Head of School, Capital City Public Charter School), in discussion with coauthor Sarah Fiarman, Friday, June 30, 2017.
3. Laina Cox (Middle School Principal, Capital City Public Charter School), in discussion with coauthor Sarah Fiarman, Friday, July 14, 2017.
4. Amanda Kemp, "How to Have a Difficult Conversation About Race (without losing your voice or your cool!)," webinar, February 21, 2018.
5. Glenn E. Singleton, *Courageous Conversations About Race: A Field Guide for Achieving Equity in Schools* (Thousand Oaks, CA: Corwin, 2015), 70.
6. Jay Smooth, "How I Learned to Stop Worrying and Love Discussing Race," TED talk, November 15, 2011, https://www.youtube.com/watch?v=MbdxeFcQtaU.

Chapter 6

1. M. Phillips, "What Makes Schools Effective? A Comparison of the Relationships of Communitarian Climate and Academic Climate to Mathematics Achievement and Attendance During Middle School," *American Educational Research Journal* 34, no. 4 (1997): 633–62, doi:10.2307/1163352.
2. S. D. McMahon, J. Wernsman, and D. S. Rose, "The Relation of Classroom Environment and School Belonging to Academic Self-Efficacy Among Urban Fourth and Fifth Grade Students," *The Elementary School Journal* 109, no. 3 (2009): 267–81.
3. A. Cabrera, A. Nora, and P. Terenzini, "Campus Racial Climate and the Adjustment of Students to College: A Comparison Between White Students and African-American Students," *The Journal of Higher Education* 70 (1999): 134–60; A. Nora and A. F. Cabrera, "The Role of Perceptions in Prejudice and Discrimination and the Adjustment of Minority Students to College," *The Journal of Higher Education* 67 (1996): 119–48.
4. Ibid.
5. R. Ferguson and R. Ramsdell, "Tripod Classroom-Level Student Perceptions as Measures of Teaching Effectiveness," 2011, http://www.gse.harvard.edu/ncte/ news/.
6. Eddie Moore Jr., Ali Michael, and Marguerite W. Penick-Parks, *The Guide for White Women Who Teach Black Boys* (Thousand Oaks, CA: Corwin, 2018), 74.
7. Ibid.

Chapter 7

1. Elena Aguilar, "Teacher to Student Interactions Tracking Tool," *Bright Morning*, http://brightmorningteam.com/wp-content/uploads/2017/09/T-S-Interactions-Tracking-Tool-Example.pdf.

2. S. Kendal, P. Keeley, and P. Callery, "Young People's Preferences for Emotional Well-Being Support in High School: A Focus Group Study," *Journal of Child and Adolescent Psychiatric Nursing* 24, no. 1 (2011): 245–53.

3. Mihir Zaveri, "A Manager Asked a Black Man to Leave the Pool at His Own Apartment Complex," *New York Times*, July 12, 2018, https://www.nytimes.com/2018/07/12/us/black-man-asked-pool-incident.html; Daniel Victor, "'All I Did Was Be Black': Police Are Called on College Student Eating Lunch," *New York Times*, August 2, 2018, https://www.nytimes.com/2018/08/02/us/black-smith-college-student-oumou-kanoute.html; Kristine Phillips, "A Black Lawmaker Was Canvassing Door to Door in Her District. A Constituent Called 911," *Washington Post*, July 6, 2018, https://www.washingtonpost.com/news/post-nation/wp/2018/07/05/a-black-lawmaker-was-campaigning-door-to-door-in-her-district-a-constituent-called-911/?utm_term=.2f9953bf127a; Britton O'Daly, "Yale Responds After Black Student Reported for Napping in Common Room," *Yale Daily News*, May 10, 2018, https://yaledailynews.com/blog/2018/05/10/yale-responds-after-black-student-reported-for-napping-in-common-room/; Elizabeth Dias, John Eligon, and Richard A. Oppel Jr., "Philadelphia Starbucks Arrests, Outrageous to Some, Are Everyday Life for Others," *New York Times*, April 17, 2018, https://www.nytimes.com/2018/04/17/us/starbucks-arrest-philadelphia.html.

4. Jennifer Eberhardt et al., "Seeing Black: Race, Crime, and Visual Processing," *Journal of Personality and Social Psychology* 87, no. 6 (2004): 876–93.

5. D. J. Losen, "Discipline Policies, Successful Schools, and Racial Justice" (Boulder, CO: National Education Policy Center), 2011, http://nepc.colorado.edu/publication/discipline-policies, retrieved August 12, 2018.

6. J. Okonofua and J. Eberhardt, "Two Strikes: Race and the Disciplining of Young Students," *Psychological Science* 26, no. 5 (2015): 617–24.

7. R. Skiba, R., Michael, A. Nardo, and R. Peterson, "The Color of Discipline: Sources of Racial and Gender Disproportionality," *The Urban Review* 34, no. 4 (2002): 317–42.

8. Ibid, 343–44.

9. Ibid., 317–42.

10. Amanda E. Lewis and John B. Diamond, *Despite the Best Intentions: How Racial Inequality Thrives in Good Schools* (New York: Oxford University Press, 2017).

11. Ibid., 88.

12. Ibid., 45.

13. Ibid., 111.

14. Jessica Nordell, "A Fix for Gender Bias in Health Care?," *New York Times*, January 11, 2017, https://www.nytimes.com/2017/01/11/opinion/a-fix-for-gender-bias-in-health-care-check.html.

15. In his book *Solving Disproportionality and Achieving Equity: A Leader's Guide to Using Data to Change Hearts and Minds*, educator Edward Fergus provides formulas for creating risk indexes like these as a way to shine a light on areas for further investigation. Edward Fergus, *Solving Disproportionality and Achieving Equity: A Leader's Guide to Using Data to Change Hearts and Minds* (Thousand Oaks, CA: Corwin, 2016).

16. R. Skiba and K. Knesting, "Zero Tolerance, Zero Evidence: An Analysis of School Disciplinary Practice," *New Directions for Student Leadership* 92 (2001: 17–43).

Chapter 8

1. Christopher Emdin, *For White Folks Who Teach in the Hood . . . and the Rest of Y'all Too: Reality Pedagogy and Urban Education* (Boston: Beacon Press, 2016), 170–71.
2. Donna Deyhle, "What is on Your Classroom Wall? Problematic Posters," in *Everyday Antiracism: Getting Real About Race in School*, ed. Mica Pollock (New York: The New Press, 2008), 191–94.
3. Adrienne Rich, *Blood, Bread, and Poetry: Selected Prose 1979–1985* (New York: Norton, 1986), 198–201.
4. Emily Style, "Curriculum as Window and Mirror," *Social Science Record* 33, no. 2 (1996): 35–45.
5. From an EL Education internal resource for auditing texts used in the curriculum.
6. TNTP, "The Opportunity Myth: What Students Can Show Us About How School is Letting Them Down, and How to Fix It" (New York: TNTP, 2018).
7. C. Clotfelter, H. Ladd, and J. Vigdor, "Who Teaches Whom? Race and the Distribution of Novice Teachers," *Economics of Education Review* 24 (2005): 377–92.
8. D. Kalogrides, S. Loeb, and T. Beteille, "Systematic Sorting: Teacher Characteristics and Class Assignments," *Sociology of Education* 86, no. 2 (2012): 103–23.
9. Amanda E. Lewis and John B. Diamond, *Despite the Best Intentions: How Racial Inequality Thrives in Good Schools* (New York: Oxford University Press, 2017).

Chapter 9

1. Robert Kegan and Lisa Lahey, *How the Way We Talk Can Change the Way We Work* (San Francisco: Jossey-Bass, 2001), 108–10.
2. Amanda E. Lewis and John B. Diamond, *Despite the Best Intentions: How Racial Inequality Thrives in Good Schools* (New York: Oxford University Press, 2017).
3. Sarah E. Fiarman, *Becoming a School Principal: Learing to Lead, Leading to Learn* (Cambridge, MA: Harvard Education Press, 2015).
4. Kegan and Lahey, *How the Way We Talk Can Change the Way We Work*, 108–10.
5. S. Reardon, J. Robinson, and E. Weathers, "Patterns and Trends in Racial/Ethnic and Socioeconomic Academic Achievement Gaps," *Handbook of Research in Education Finance and Policy* (Abingdon, UK: Routledge, 2008), 497–516.

Chapter 10

1. Ronald A. Heifetz and Martin Linsky, *Leadership on the Line: Staying Alive Through the Dangers of Leading* (Boston: Harvard Business School Press, 2002).

2. Patrisse Cullors and Robert Ross, interview by Krista Tibbet, *On Being*, Krista Tibbet Public Productions, February 18, 2016.

3. Douglas Stone, Bruce Patton, and Sheila Heen, *Difficult Conversations: How to Discuss What Matters Most* (New York: Penguin Books, 2000); Carol S. Dweck, *Mindset: The New Psychology of Success* (New York: Random House, 2006).

4. Robin DiAngelo, *What Does It Mean to Be White?: Developing White Racial Literacy* (New York: Peter Lang Publishing, Inc, 2016).

5. The Odyssey School of Denver.

6. Laina Cox (Middle School Principal, Capital City Public Charter School), in discussion with coauthor Sarah Fiarman, Friday, July 14, 2017.

Acknowledgments

At various times while writing this book, colleagues have pointed out that it's rare for a black author and a white author to be able to write a book together about race. "Look around," one professor said. "You don't see many examples of black and white coauthorship in this field." After working on this book together for several years, we can confirm the inherent difficulties in this task. For this reason, we first want to thank each other. We're grateful that we persevered through challenges in the service of writing something we hope will help our colleagues and ultimately improve the experience of all students.

At one point in our work together, Tracey described some of the dynamics playing out between us. We were sitting at a seafood restaurant that used large pieces of brown butcher paper as disposable tablecloths. In the middle of a conversation about chapter revisions, Tracey pulled out a pen and started drawing on the butcher paper. He drew two identical pie charts, each showing one small section of the pie highlighted. He explained that the pie charts represented the way we each thought about our collaboration. "The problem," Tracey said, labeling the smaller section of the first pie, "is that you think that this represents the racism in our relationship and this [pointing to the larger section] represents the misunderstandings in our relationship." He then moved his pen to the second pie chart and labeled the pieces the opposite way, explaining, "And I think it's the other way around."

As in any relationship, neither of us perceived the situation completely accurately. Our journey through the writing process included many courageous conversations about race and racism, philosophical disagreements, and moments of frustration. At times, misunderstandings played more of a role in our work together. At other times, racism clouded our path and made it difficult to move forward.

We think this is likely true for most cross-race collaborations, including those we hope take root in schools leading anti-racist work. For this reason, we want to model in our acknowledgments a recognition of the extra work people of color do in cross-race collaborations. In our collaboration, we both persevered through misunderstandings, but only one of us had to carry the burden of explaining Sarah's bias to her while at the same time experiencing its negative impact. We could not have written this book without Tracey's willingness to continually return to the table to teach Sarah about her own racism—her own unconscious racial bias. Countless people of color teach their colleagues in schools every day without ever being recognized or compensated and without any acknowledgment of the emotional toll. We thank them, too.

Our editor Caroline Chauncey steadfastly supported our collaboration. Caroline's superpower is an ability to make authors feel capable of tackling challenges that seem insurmountable. She provides encouragement and critical feedback in just the right proportions. We are grateful for her wise editorial advice and her patience throughout the process.

Many other people helped us write this book, some directly, others indirectly. We are grateful to our friends, family, and colleagues who carefully read parts or all of the draft: Bob Algozzine; Devyn Spence Benson; Ruth Charney; Norma Elliott; Sidney, Janell, and Rebecca Fiarman; David Jacobson; Laurie McDonnell; and Peggy McIntosh. These readers provided wise and practical feedback that helped us return to the draft with fresh insights and renewed motivation.

Many people with whom we have worked helped us shape concepts in this book. They asked questions or offered perspectives that informed our writing. The list is too long to print, but we would like to particularly thank Bela Bhasin, Christina Brown; Cameron Browne; Sarah Bruhn, Jeanie Cho; Laina Cox; Gail Cruise-Roberson, Emmy Howe, and the National SEED Project; Cesar Cruz; Karen Dresden; Carlos Duque; Manuel Fernandez; Michael Figueroa; Pat Finley; Annice Fisher; Sarah Foleno; Tracey Gordon; GP Task Force members; Kathy Greeley; Cyndi Gueswel; Seng and Peter Keo; Zaretta Hammond; Tremain Holloway; MyTien Huynh; Claudie Jean-Baptiste; Michelle Johnson; Kristina Kyles-Smith; Jeana Marinelli; Damon McCord; Eddie Moore Jr.; Michelle Navarre; Jo Quest-Neubert; Ellen Royse; Ruby Sales; Michael Scott; Glenn Singleton; Lee Teitel; Christina Villarreal; Judith Williams; Ayana Wilson; Rafael Zavala.

We are grateful to the many people who encouraged us along this journey, and we want to especially call out those who took care of us in different ways during this book's birth. Tracey is grateful to Devyn Spence Benson for her thoughtfulness, care, and encouragement during the writing process as well as listening to hours upon hours of Sarah and Tracey discuss the book on Google Hangout. Sarah is grateful to Rachel Curtis (for oranges, insight, chocolate, and cheerleading); Laurie McDonnell (for listening and providing wisdom and clarity every step of the way); Tom McDonnell (for just-right cards); Emily, Kevin, Maya, Alex, and Calvin Qazilbash (for sharing their family); John Tyler (for inspiration, over and over again).

We also want to express our love for family members who have nourished us during this book-writing process. Sarah thanks her sister, Rebecca Fiarman, and parents, Sidney and Janell Fiarman, for a lifetime of selfless support and love. Tracey thanks his wife, Dr. Devyn Spence Benson, for her love, encouragement, and unyielding support. Tracey also thanks his son, Camoren; brothers, Ola, Tristan, and Troy; sisters, Shareen and Sabrina; and parents, Louise and Olalekan, for their support and inspiration; and his in-laws, Mr. and Mrs. Spence, Uncle Jay and Aunt Gail, for their encouragement and celebration.

About the Authors

Tracey A. Benson is an assistant professor of educational leadership at the University of North Carolina at Charlotte. He received his Ed.L.D. in education leadership from the Harvard Graduate School of Education and master's of school administration from the University of North Carolina–Chapel Hill. He has been a classroom teacher at the elementary level, vice principal at the middle school level, professional development specialist at the district level, and principal at the high school level. He has served as a school and district leader in Texas, North Carolina, Florida, and Massachusetts. As a high school principal, Tracey eliminated inequitable teaching and discipline practices, partnered with local organizations, and mentored struggling students as a means of addressing racial and socioeconomic inequities within the schools and surrounding communities. His efforts in leading for social justice significantly decreased the suspension rates of students of color and students from low socioeconomic backgrounds, while increasing the academic achievement of all students who attended the schools where he served.

As a doctoral candidate, Tracey cofounded the Harvard Graduate School of Education's first Ethnic Studies course. The course sought to provide students with a counternarrative to traditional US history by highlighting the histories and experiences of Native Americans, African Americans, Latinos/as, and Asian Americans. Tracey also coauthored a teaching case, "Lessons from Ferguson: Leadership in Times of Civil Unrest," aimed at helping schools and school districts understand the nuances of structural racism. After publishing the teaching case with Harvard Education Press, Tracey, along with his co-case writer, traveled nationally to school districts, organizations, and conferences to present their work and facilitate discussions aimed at helping participants understand the meaning of structural racism and identifying purposeful practices in their own communities for overturning it.

Tracey has committed his career to leading for change, courageously addressing entrenched practices that impede lifetime outcomes of students of color. As an assistant professor of educational leadership, Tracey's research focuses on analyzing the relationship between educational leadership and dismantling structural racism in K–12 schools. He examines and offers best practices for how educational leaders can lead for social justice and advocate for racial equity.

In addition to coauthoring the teaching case, Tracey has authored many other pieces, including, "Leadership Amidst Racial Trauma and Unrest: UNC Charlotte's Response to the Shooting of Keith Scott" (*Journal of Cases in Educational Leadership*); "Stemming Teacher Shortages: A Community Apprenticeship Model" (a chapter in *From Head to Heart*); and "To Google Translate or not? Newcomer Latino Communities in the Middle" (*Middle School Journal*).

Sarah E. Fiarman is the director of leadership development with EL Education, a national, nonprofit organization partnering with schools and districts to ensure all students have access to challenging, engaging, and empowering learning. Sarah became an educator out of a commitment to teach anti-racism to all students and ensure that black and brown students received the excellent education they were too often denied. Over the years, her aims have shifted to include a focus on helping white people (starting with herself) see their role in perpetuating racial inequities and their responsibility to continually work to change these behaviors.

A former public school teacher and principal, Sarah is the author of *Becoming a School Principal: Learning to Lead, Leading to Learn* and a coauthor of *Instructional Rounds in Education: A Network Approach to Improving Teaching and Learning*. Sarah is also a contributing author of books from the Data Wise Project at Harvard Graduate School of Education.

While teaching, Sarah was a National Board Certified Teacher, Responsive Classroom Consulting Teacher, and trained facilitator with Seeking Educational Equity and Diversity. She co-led the parent-teacher anti-racism/anti-bias discussion group and, with her teaching team, was awarded the Cambridge Peace and Justice award. As a principal, she was awarded a Lynch Leadership Academy Fellowship through Boston College, and in 2013, the *Boston Globe* rated her school the "#1 Dream School in Massachusetts" based primarily on student academic growth scores. She served as lecturer and director of field placement in the School Leadership Program at Harvard Graduate School of Education, where she also cofounded and co-led the faculty group discussing race and racism. She received her EdD from Harvard Graduate School of Education in administration, planning, and social policy.

Index